D0871354

GREAT
MORAL DILEMMAS

In Literature, Past and Present

RELIGION AND CIVILIZATION SERIES

RELIGION AND CIVILIZATION SERIES

GREAT
MORAL DILEMMAS

In Literature, Past and Present

EDITED BY

R. M. MacIver

LIEBER PROFESSOR EMERITUS OF POLITICAL PHILOSOPHY
AND SOCIOLOGY, COLUMBIA UNIVERSITY

Published by

The INSTITUTE for RELIGIOUS and SOCIAL STUDIES

Distributed by

HARPER & BROTHERS

NEW YORK

PRINTED IN THE UNITED STATES OF AMERICA
BY THE VAIL-BALLOU PRESS, INC., BINGHAMTON, N. Y.

This volume contains the series of luncheon addresses delivered at The Institute for Religious and Social Studies of The Jewish Theological Seminary of America during the winter of 1954–1955.

Each chapter in this volume represents solely the individual opinion of the author. Neither the Institute nor the editor assumes responsibility for the views expressed. We have been fortunate enough to enlist a group of authors each of whom has distinctive knowledge in his own field, and the Institute is indeed grateful for the generous way in which they have responded to its invitation.

This is a Jacob Ziskind Memorial publication.

CONTENTS

I. IN MODERN LITERATURE

I

THE TERGIVERSATION OF HERMAN WOUK

(*The Caine Mutiny*)

BY

ROBERT BIERSTEDT

The Caine Mutiny was published on March 19, 1951. After a somewhat sluggish start it found its way to the best-seller list of the *New
York Times* and to the surprise of almost everyone, including a pub-
lisher who had rejected the manuscript, it remained there for one
hundred twenty-three weeks. Domestic sales in various editions are
well over the three million mark. It has been translated into sixteen
foreign languages; it has been syndicated in forty-one American
newspapers; it has been distributed by no less than four book clubs;
and its author has been awarded a Pulitzer Prize. *The Caine Mutiny
Court Martial,* a play prepared by the author himself, opened on
Broadway in January of 1954 and is still [November, 1954] playing
to capacity audiences. The movie opened at the Capitol Theater in
New York on June 24, and by now it is impossible to estimate the
number of millions of people who have joined the crew of the Caine
and who have participated, however vicariously, in one of the best
advertised "mutinies" in history.

We have here a phenomenon which has one set of implications for
Madison Avenue, however, and quite another for this quiet seminary
on Morningside Heights.[1] For *The Caine Mutiny,* whatever one
thinks of it as a publishing success, is a work of considerable literary
merit. It is a book, moreover, which introduces an interesting moral
issue. This, of course, is one of the functions of literature, and the

[1] The Jewish Theological Seminary of America, where the chapter was originally
presented as a lecture.

greater the literature, as this entire series exemplifies, the more imposing the moral problem. Although the rank of the book as a work of art does not directly concern us, we should be disposed to argue that a moral flaw in its structure, if such it be, is relevant to an esthetic judgment. That the novel does contain a moral flaw is the case I want to propose and this in spite of a personal admiration for Herman Wouk which is both wholehearted and humble. The flaw is one which no amount of admiration can altogether subdue, no casuistry wholly conceal.

The extraordinary popularity of *The Caine Mutiny,* in book and play and movie, renders unnecessary a recapitulation of the plot. As an aid to recollection, however, we may reintroduce the cast of characters so that the problems they severally and individually confront can claim our attention.

The protagonist of the novel is Willie Keith, a Princeton man and sometime singer in night clubs who aspires to a professorship in Romance languages. (It is, we are encouraged to believe, a genteel profession and one well suited to the otherwise idle rich.) In the course of his tour of naval duty Willie greatly matures and as we leave him at the book's end we suspect, with some apprehension, that he may turn out to be a professor after all. In the book, however, Willie serves an important purpose. It is his eyes through which we observe the mutiny on the Caine and further, as Wouk says, "the event turned on his personality as the massive door of a vault turns on a small jewel bearing." When, at the height of the storm, the two officers of the Caine, the captain and the executive officer, give contradictory orders to the helmsman, the latter, Stilwell, appeals in real fear to Willie, then on duty as Officer of the Deck. It is apparent that if Willie, at this tense moment, had supported the captain instead of the executive officer, the latter's attempt to relieve his skipper would have failed. In this sense, the author is saying, Willie is essential to the plot; this is his *raison d'être.*

The importance of a single individual in the causation of a complex event in human affairs is always open to question, as Tolstoy has so supremely taught us. Given the circumstances, it may be argued that the result was inevitable and that Willie had no more to do with it—and no less—than any other member of the fated company. But historiography and fiction are two different enterprises. The novelist's art requires him to accept a theory which a sociologist is ordinarily tempted to reject, that is, the heroic (or diabolic) theory of history. We may readily concede to Wouk, therefore, that Willie was not only important but essential to the mutiny of the Caine. At the same time we ought to note, perhaps, that all of the officers of the Caine supported Maryk in his relief of Queeg, and this without further question or controversy.

The second officer to engage our attention is Philip Spencer Queeg, named no doubt after Midshipman Philip Spencer, one of three men actually hanged for mutiny in 1842, the only mutiny recorded in the naval history of the United States, and that, too, incidentally, a dubious one. Lieutenant Commander Queeg is the captain of the Caine. He is also "regular Navy" and the Articles for the Government of the Navy are his only Bible and his only Law. He is more than a disciplinarian; he is a martinet. He possesses that combination of qualities which usually makes for success in any bureaucracy and for failure everywhere else. While martinets and myrmidons may be conspicuous in military organizations, they can be found, of course, in all the organizations of society. Wouk need not apologize therefore to the Navy for drawing this kind of portrait of one of its officers, although his compunction to do so is unaccountably clear. The normal curve of probability has ends as well as a middle, and in any group as large as the Navy some persons will find their places at the extremities of the curve.

We learn very early that as a ship's handler Queeg is clumsy and inept. His seamanship is not only faulty; it is often dangerous. At the time of the typhoon it is clear, although Wouk later tries to compromise the picture, that he is doing everything wrong. His refusal to come into the wind, to ballast his tanks, and to turn the depth charges on "Safe" all increase the hazards to his ship. He fails to do what a reasonably prudent and capable seaman would do on the ground that standing orders are still standing and that not even a typhoon justifies the slightest departure, or exercise of initiative.

But Queeg is not, in other circumstances, a "book-officer" at all.

He illegally transports back to the States a consignment of liquor for his own personal use and then extorts the cost of it from Willie when, because of his own mistakes, it is lost overboard. On several occasions he submits to his superiors reports which stray rather considerably from the truth in the direction of self-justification, and he offers, in the instance of the "mutiny" itself, to erase and rewrite the rough logs of the ship. This last, for obvious reasons, is an exceedingly serious offense against naval regulations.

The issue of cowardice as affecting Queeg is one which the author treats with insight and skill. The captain never stays on the exposed side of the bridge when the ship is under fire. In one case he fails to return enemy fire when he has an opportunity to do so, and instead moves the Caine out of range as rapidly as possible. In escorting assault boats to the beach at Kwajalein he runs far ahead of them, drops a dyemarker indicating the line of departure, and then hastily runs again for safety. This last incident wins him the name, "Old Yellowstain," among his subordinate officers, and the "Yellow," of course, stands for more than the color of the dye. For the reader at least, Wouk clearly, steadily, and consistently establishes, beyond any lingering possibility of skepticism, that Queeg is a coward.

Queeg, however, is not on trial, and the charge of cowardice which Willie Keith's testimony so clearly implies has no legal stature. The defense attorney, Greenwald, denies that Queeg is guilty of cowardice, on the ground that no man certified by the Navy as qualified for command could possibly be guilty of so heinous a charge. On the contrary, if Queeg's actions seem to suggest cowardice, they must instead be attributed to a mental affliction. The testimony of three psychiatrists that Queeg's condition is not disabling suffers heavily under cross-examination and particularly when Greenwald maintains that the court is better qualified than a board of medical examiners to estimate the stresses of command.

Finally, of course, Queeg convicts himself by going to pieces on the witness stand, repeating tiresome trivialities over and over to the point of echolalia and clicking his little steel balls together as his case disintegrates. The captain and his creator together have convinced us all that the "mutiny" was justified and that Maryk, the executive officer, is innocent even of the lesser charge of "conduct to the prejudice of good order and discipline." It is a dramatic, colorful, and exciting story, and at the climax, as throughout, only one conclusion is possible.

Lieutenant Stephen Maryk, who relieves Queeg and who thus becomes the defendant in the court-martial action, is not so fully rounded nor so richly detailed as the other officers. A fisherman before the war who now aspires to transfer to the Regular Navy, he is an extraordinarily able seaman. He is more than that. He is a decent, honest, and courageous citizen. As executive officer under Queeg he is caught between the parlous captain and the reluctant crew, and he performs the duties of this trying and essentially ambivalent position with distinction, retaining both the trust of his subordinates and the confidence of the skipper. As the situation is constructed this would seem to be an impossible task, but Maryk somehow manages to accomplish it. He relieves Queeg only after he is convinced that the ship is in its last extremity and that the captain, in panic, has lost touch with the reality of the raging seas.

Maryk is not stupid, however, and to suggest that he is the mere pawn of Keefer, cowed by Keefer's superior intellect and supposedly superior insight into the dark recesses of the human mind, is to do him a disservice. Maryk may not know the technical language of psychoanalysis, but he knows an incompetent mariner when he sees one, and Wouk leaves no doubt that he does see one on the bridge of the Caine at the height of the typhoon. Maryk acts throughout—and especially in the action for which he is court-martialed—with vigor and decision. To suggest that he is at any time motivated by disloyalty, is to distort the image of a character which the author has carefully, if briefly, constructed.

Lieutenant Thomas Keefer, of course, is the Cassius of the Caine. An intellectual and a writer, Keefer induces Maryk to keep a medical log on the captain and explains the captain's symptoms as they appear. It is Keefer who is always somewhere else when unpleasant decisions have to be made; it is Keefer who displays both moral and physical cowardice; and it is Keefer finally who betrays his friend Maryk on the witness stand. Keefer is conscious of his weaknesses, however, and with a curious candor even confesses to them. At least one critic—Granville Hicks—has regarded Wouk's treatment of Keefer as an assault upon intellectuals and as one more indication of the anti-intellectualism of our time. This is a complaint which we shall consider in the sequel.

We come finally to Lieutenant Barney Greenwald, the only one of the five officers who was not a member of the Caine's company and who serves instead as Maryk's counsel. He appears first as a quiet but arrogant individual who thinks, on the one hand, that Steve Maryk and Willie Keith "deserve to get slugged" and, on the other, that only a "halfway intelligent defense" will suffice to get them off. He hesitates at first to take the case and then expresses himself so dogmatically against his own prospective clients that one might question the wisdom of his superior in permitting him to do so. "I just don't want to defend these Caine people," he says. "Captain Queeg obviously is not crazy. The psychiatrist's report proves it. These fools find a paragraph in Navy Regs that gives them ideas, and they gang up on a skipper who's mean and stupid—as a lot of skippers are—and make jackasses of themselves, and put a ship out of action. I'm a damn good lawyer and a very expensive one, and I don't see contributing my services to get them acquitted."

This speech attracts our attention for several reasons. In the first place the reader by this time has thoroughly identified himself with the defendants and like them he is desperately in need of an adequate defense against the recommended charge of mutiny. It comes as a disappointment therefore that the attorney who will serve in this capacity has so enthusiastically prejudged the case. His prejudgment might possibly be excused on the ground that he is talking only to two other lawyers, but, on the other hand, one of them, Challee, is scheduled, as judge advocate, to be his opponent at the trial. But even worse, it is a prejudgment which stems from ignorance. When Greenwald makes this remark he knows nothing whatever about the events which occurred on the Caine and has no warrant for assuming that it is merely a case of discontented men "ganging up" on a "mean and stupid skipper."

Greenwald is also wrong in his anticipation of the character of

Maryk. The person he expects to see is the college radical of the thirties—thin, dark, sensitive, *intellectual,* antimilitary in general and antiNavy in particular, possibly even a Communist. Maryk, of course, is none of these things, and so Greenwald receives his first surprise.

Finally we learn—in the book but not in the movie—that Greenwald is a Jew, and we are informed that he therefore has an especial reason to appreciate the United States Navy. In the movie Greenwald is merely a loyal American who supports, as "intellectuals" apparently do not, the importance of the peacetime Navy.

This, then, is the cast of characters. To this cast we may now add Herman Wouk, the man who wrote the book. Wouk sees the action which occurred on the Caine as a rebellion against authority, a rebellion he first considers justified and then, inconsistently and unaccountably, unjustified. Mutiny, of course, is rebellion of a high order since it is a challenge to the authority of a captain of a ship at sea. We are prepared to concede that such authority is and must be almost absolute. Indeed, it has been remarked that a captain on his bridge is the closest a civilized society ever comes to an absolute monarch. It is a situation in which only monarchy can work. Obedience to such authority must be instantaneous and unquestioned; it is an authority recognized, protected, and supported both by naval law and by long maritime tradition. The perils of the sea require special vigilance, and special rules, in consequence, have arisen to cope with them.

Now as Wouk tells us himself, there was no genuine mutiny on the Caine. We have here no "flashing of cutlasses, no captain in chains," no criminal sailors seizing the ship in order to pursue their own designs. After Maryk relieves the captain the structure of authority remains precisely what it was before. The functions of the crew remain the same and so also does the mission of the ship. Particular individuals no longer occupy the same places in the structure, but the authority itself is both intact and unchallenged.

Nor is it a mutiny in another sense. As Greenwald immediately recognizes, "There's no question of force or violence or disrespect." Maryk even apologizes to Queeg at the moment of relief, using the following formula, "Captain, I'm sorry, sir, you're a sick man. I am temporarily relieving you of command of this ship, under Article 184 of *Navy Regulations*." Article 184 reads as follows:

It is conceivable that most unusual and extraordinary circumstances may arise in which the relief from duty of a commanding officer by a subordinate becomes necessary, either by placing him under arrest or on the sick list; but such action shall never be taken without the approval of the Navy Department or other appropriate higher authority, except when reference to such higher authority is undoubtedly impracticable because of the delay involved or for other clearly obvious reason. Such reference must set forth all facts in the case, and the reasons for the recommendation, with particular regard to the degree of urgency involved.

Article 185 says in addition, and in part:

In order that a subordinate officer, acting upon his own initiative, may be vindicated for relieving a commanding officer from duty, the situation must be obvious and clear, and must admit of the single conclusion that the retention of command by such commanding officer will seriously and irretrievably prejudice the public interests.

These passages indicate that the authority to relieve a commanding officer under certain conditions is clearly present in naval law and that Maryk's action is therefore no challenge to authority. Indeed, Maryk invokes the relevant authority at the moment of relief. In all that has preceded, Wouk has demonstrated that the situation is "obvious and clear" and admits of the single conclusion "which a reasonable, prudent, and experienced officer would regard as a necessary consequence from the facts thus determined to exist." The notion that Maryk's action is somehow a rebellion against authority, is one which is susceptible to serious question. The action must, of course, be justified and this is the task to which Greenwald devotes himself, with the unwitting assistance of Queeg himself, in the famous trial scenes. We all rejoice therefore when a sensible verdict is sensibly reached. From the facts which the author has given us, not only in court but during the long cruise of the Caine itself, acquittal is the only possible conclusion.

So now the trial is over, the case concluded, the novel finished. Maryk's acquittal in the confusion and tumult of war is itself a potent compliment to the Navy. We can take pride in a military organization in which the exercise of authority is not unaccompanied by compassion. The Navy we see in Wouk's book is no Prussian organization, placing discipline above all other considerations, including the safety of its ships and the lives of its men. Our suspense during the trial is sustained by our suspicion of the Navy; now we discover with relief that the suspicion is unjustified, that the Navy, too, can take account of human frailty and human need. The dinner party to celebrate the verdict and to pay tribute to Greenwald for his defense of Maryk promises to be an anticlimax. For us, the readers, justice has triumphed—as we were afraid it would not—and right has prevailed.

But now something happens which alters the complexion of the book and reverses its thesis. The victory party does not finish the novel but instead destroys the consistency of the plot and mars the moral integrity of the author's achievement. Something happens which we are induced to call the tergiversation of Herman Wouk.

The scene is the victory dinner, called and paid for by Keefer as a double celebration, first for the acquittal and second for the acceptance of his novel by a publishing house. In the midst of the alcoholic gaiety Greenwald stumbles drunkenly into the room and, as the hero of the trial, is called upon to speak. In response he asks first about Keefer's book, a war novel, and then—incredibly—says, "It suddenly seems to me that if I wrote a war novel I'd try to make a hero out of Old Yellowstain." He is quite serious. To explain the reason for making Queeg a hero he invokes his little old Jewish mother. When the "Germans started running out of soap and figured, well it's time to come over and melt down old Mrs. Greenwald—who's gonna stop them? Not her boy Barney. Can't stop a Nazi with a lawbook. So I dropped the lawbooks and ran to learn how to fly. Stout fellow. Meantime, and it took a year and a half before I was any good, who was keeping Mama out of the soap dish? Captain Queeg."

In this maudlin scene we are suddenly asked to believe that Queeg, in contrast to everything we have known of him before, is a hero; that Keefer, who gets the champagne in his face, is a villain; and that Maryk, in relieving the captain, has committed an unforgivable crime. Here is transvaluation with a vengeance! Why has Wouk done this? For many pages we have followed him in good faith, believing that Queeg was indeed afflicted with a mental aberration (remember, for example, the strawberry incident), believing that he was at bottom a coward who preferred not to face the enemy, believing, finally, that he was wholly incapacitated by fear at the height of the typhoon and unable in consequence to save his ship. We believe that Maryk is the savior of the Caine and of the lives of the men, because Wouk, with a superior artistry, has convinced us that this is so. We have given him our total attention throughout and now, without warning, he is telling us that he has deceived us, that Maryk and the other officers are guilty, that Queeg is to be praised for having joined the peacetime Navy, and that authority ought to be upheld in any cause however ignoble and in any person however cowardly, crazy, or incompetent. The story for him has become as simple as the assertion in the Book of Luke (7:8), "For I also am a man set under authority, having under me soldiers, and I say unto one, Go, and he goeth; and to another Come, and he cometh."

Wouk is telling us in addition that he is sorry he has written the story the way he has and that he, too, deserves an appropriate punishment. He will now do penance and write the remainder of his book from an opposite point of view. This opposition, amounting to a contradiction, is expressed in the words of the reviewing authority, which disapproves the acquittal of Maryk, which "believes the specification proved beyond a reasonable doubt," and which continues:

There is in this case a miscarriage of justice whereby an officer escapes punishment for a serious offense and a dangerous precedent has been established. The fact that the ship was in hazard does not mitigate, but rather intensifies the responsibility of the accused. It is at times of hazard most of all that the line of naval discipline should be held rigidly, especially by senior officers on a ship . . . A ship can have only one commanding officer, appointed by the government, and to remove him in an irregular manner without referring the matter to the highest available authority is an act exceeding the powers of a second-in-command. This doctrine is emphasized, not weakened, by the description in Articles 184,

185, and 186 of the exceedingly rare circumstances in which exception may be made, and the intentions of the Navy Department to this effect are therein expressed with the utmost clarity and vigor.

Finally, Willie himself accepts the thesis that Maryk was acquitted by legal trickery. In a letter to May Wynn he accuses himself and Maryk of disloyalty and suggests that they transferred to Queeg the hatred they should have felt for Hitler and the Japanese. The reverse rationalization of the letter concludes with the following remarkable recommendation to serve authority with a blind obedience: "The idea is, once you get an incompetent ass of a skipper—and it's a chance of war—there's nothing to do but serve him as though he were the wisest and the best, cover his mistakes, keep the ship going, and bear up." And when he reads the words of the reviewing authority he says, "Well, I concur too. That makes it unanimous."

But Willie is wrong. The verdict is not unanimous. It is for us, the readers, to render judgment and most of us, I suspect, will support the court against the author's belated change of mind. We need no legal trickery, no courtroom prestidigitation, to show that the novelist has now done us—and himself—a disservice, and that his final philosophy of authority requires reexamination and rejection.

A number of reasons weigh in the balance and encourage this conclusion. The first of these is that not even so competent a writer as Herman Wouk is able to refute in roughly fifty pages a point of view he has taken four hundred and fifty pages to advance. What he has done he cannot now undo. Having convinced us at length that Queeg is guilty of both incompetence and cowardice, he cannot now convince us in so short a space that Queeg, on the contrary, is a hero who is motivated throughout only by his own conceptions of what is good for the Navy and that these conceptions are valid. Such a transformation does not square with the yellowstain incident, the extortion for the lost liquor, the case of the missing strawberries, or the captain's paralysis during the storm.

Similarly, Maryk, limned for us throughout as an able and decent citizen, stands now accused of stupidity and of conduct to the prejudice of good order and discipline. After observing him for many, many pages and many, many months at sea it is simply not possible to concur in this opinion. Our author, however, is adamant, and therefore has to punish Maryk. He may be only half-guilty, as Greenwald tells him in the climactic scene, but, on the other hand, he is only half-acquitted, too. His chances of transfer to the Regular Navy are now forfeit and he is in fact demoted to the command of an LCI (Landing Craft, Infantry). Willie, by the way, who is equally guilty, becomes the last captain of the Caine. The quick twist, in short, requires Wouk to punish Maryk and to reward Willie for what was roughly the same offense.

But even more serious is what the tergiversation does to Greenwald, whom Wouk has obviously chosen to represent his new point of view. Greenwald now assures us, in his party speech, that he got Maryk off by "phony legal tricks." Taking him at his word, is it proper for an attorney to resort to trickery in order to save a man who is at least "half-guilty" and in the process destroy another man (Queeg) to whom he now says he owes a favor? Instead of a St. George in shining armor we now have an attorney who takes a case in which he does not believe and which he wins through conscious trickery rather than conviction. By his own admission he owes a favor to Queeg but he is nevertheless responsible for consigning Queeg to the oblivion of a naval supply depot in Stuber City, Iowa. Greenwald, whom we were prepared to acclaim not only as the savior of Maryk but also as a servant of justice, now convicts himself of hypocrisy, with only the thin excuse that the wrong man was on trial. His morbid speech robs us of our respect for him. If we still have sympathy it is because we see that he, like Queeg, has symptoms of a mental affliction. The notion that Queeg, because he joined the Navy in peacetime, somehow prevented Goering from making soap out of Greenwald's mother, is about as far out of touch with reality as Queeg's search for the nonexistent key in the strawberry incident. We regretfully conclude that Greenwald has his little steel balls, too, and that they are clicking around in his head as incessantly as Queeg's click in his hand.

Wouk's change of mind involves more than a transformation in his characters. It involves in addition an incomprehensible logic. The movie critic of the *New Yorker*, John McCarten, remarks im-

patiently about Wouk's "odd notion that it was somehow heroic to
have joined the Navy in the nineteen-thirties, as the befuddled captain did, while civilians were out making fortunes on the W.P.A."
But Queeg is more than befuddled; he is wholly bereft of ideas.
There is no evidence that he has ever made a commitment to a
political or philosophical position. It is difficult to see him as a
champion of democracy, or of any other political philosophy. It is all
very well for Wouk to defend the importance of a peacetime Navy
but it is a little extravagant to contend that those who manned it
did so because they were opponents of totalitarianism or enemies of
antisemitism. Indeed, men like Queeg are wholly innocent of political
preferences and predilections. Wouk does not seem to have noticed
that Queeg would have served equally well and with equal attention
to discipline in the German Navy. His superior might as easily have
been Admiral Doenitz as Admiral Halsey. Nothing matters to him
except the shirttails of his sailors.

Our next charge against Wouk is that he does the United States
Navy a disservice in implying now that it is an organization incapable of handling the extremities of the normal probability curve,
that in personnel problems it can see only black and white and none
of the shades between, that it is permanently and inflexibly an au-
thoritarian organization. Articles 184, 185, and 186 are to be found
in Navy Regulations and we may presume at least, Wouk now to
the contrary notwithstanding, that they were put there for a purpose.
What that purpose might be, Wouk himself devotes the greater part
of his book to explaining. It is again incomprehensible therefore that
he should turn his back upon his own explanation and imply that
these articles ought not to be used, that it is somehow degrading to
the Navy even to suggest that an occasion could arise on which they
might properly be invoked. I should hazard the guess that most of us
would rather serve in Maryk's Navy than in Greenwald's, in the
Navy represented by the officers who acquitted Maryk than in the
Navy whose officers disapproved the verdict.

A final question remains. As mentioned earlier, Granville Hicks
in *The New Leader* has suggested that Wouk's treatment of Lieutenant Keefer is an assault upon intellectuals and must therefore be

regarded as one more sign of the anti-intellectualism of the times. One would like to register a dissent from this view and to defend the author against the indictment. If intellectuals occasionally stray from the canons of a strict morality, this implies merely that they share the defects and imperfections of other men. Wouk may portray Keefer's perfidy, but there is no reason for supposing that it is the perfidy of a class. Nor does Wouk maintain that there is a higher incidence of dishonesty among intellectuals than in other groups. The villains of literature come in all colors and shapes and sizes, represent every nationality, religion, and vocation, and belong to every social group.

Unfortunately, however, Wouk cannot be so easily absolved. Upon further reflection it is clear that he is objecting to Keefer not because Keefer is perfidious but because he is thoughtful. He deprecates Keefer not because of his betrayal of Maryk but because of his inclination to think. There is the clear conclusion now that if no one had done any thinking the "mutiny" would never have occurred and that Keefer, as the leading thinker, is largely to blame for the unfortunate history of the Caine. Here is an author telling us that blind obedience to authority is preferable to its rational acceptance. And this, I submit, is dangerous doctrine. An obedience which is blind is an obedience ill equipped to match the menaces of our century. This kind of obedience is the antithesis of responsible social action and ultimately the denial of an adult morality.

In these remarks I have been critical of the conclusions to which the author of *The Caine Mutiny* felt constrained to come at the end of his book. These criticisms, while relevant to both an esthetic and a moral judgment, do not detract from the esteem in which I hold both the author and his book. Nor do they reduce, in any respect but one, the distinction of Wouk's achievement. Criticism, after all, is easy, creation difficult. If my remarks are cogent they imply only that *The Caine Mutiny,* which is a very good book, could have been a much better one. They suggest that consistency is not only a canon of logic and a requirement of literature—it is also a moral virtue. And they assert without equivocation that authority differs from authoritarianism in that it always makes some attempt, however small, to satisfy the criterion of reason.

II

EFFICIENT POWER AND INEFFICIENT VIRTUE

(Bernard Shaw: *Major Barbara*)

BY

CHARLES FRANKEL

It is refreshing, in our present political mood of disenchantment and gripe, to turn back to Shaw's *Major Barbara*. It represents a kind of political thinking which now seems almost to have vanished. Our social imagination today hovers between a state of exhaustion and a state of shock. The imperatives of power—the need for defense, the need for holding actions, the need to keep an eye on the enemy—leave the imagination with very little room to play about. Things are in the saddle; and the kind of unafraid social vision which we can find in *Major Barbara,* at once tempered by the facts and building freely upon them, is no longer the vogue.

Our mood shows itself in the kind of political thinking in which we engage. On one side, a great many men are insisting that we must reaffirm certain eternal moral truths before we even look at the facts of power. On the other side, there is a kind of hardshell "realism" which insists that we must look at the facts of power alone, and take no account at all of moral ideals. On both sides, there is a curiously antipolitical strain, a fixation on the germ of corruption that lurks in every exercise of power, a suspicion that every social ideal is either a utopian vision or an unscrupulous masquerade. The Russian Revolution has been a long drawn out lesson for us in how cynicism and utopianism mix, and has left us with the feeling that no large and humane social vision can be achieved by political means. We are afraid to be taken in by shrewd operators, afraid to be taken in by a social ideal. We are convinced, quite plainly and simply, that Power

15

and Virtue do not mix. And this conviction overlays all our political thinking. *Major Barbara,* with its unashamed respect for power and its joyous commitment to a social vision, seems to come from another world.

The problem of Might *versus* Right, of efficiency *versus* moral ideals, with which *Major Barbara* deals, is in many ways the germinal problem of political philosophy. We discover its existence, I suspect, the first time we are scolded by our parents. As a problem of theory, it has to do with the justification of social authority. Is all morality merely a velvet glove over an iron fist, an ideology that simply helps those who have power to maintain that power? On its practical side, it has to do with a question of tactics. Is it better to be efficient, or is it better to be virtuous—and impotent? Is it ever possible to be both?

The weight of opinion has always been on one side—that it is better to be good than powerful, better to be right than President. But there has always been something peculiar about the perennial debate over Might *versus* Right, and this has been the simple fact that the debate has continued. Why should it continue, when opinion has so regularly been on one side of the issue? Why did Machiavelli prey on people's minds until he became the prototype for that long line of evil, but splendid, geniuses in sixteenth century poetry and drama that terminates in Iago? Why was nearly all British moral and political philosophy for two centuries a debate with a single figure, Hobbes? Why does a single statement on the side of Might have the power of a thousand statements on the side of Right? It may be a sign of man's incurable love of evil. But it may also be a sign that, in the age old struggle between the partisans of Power and the partisans of Virtue, we have steadily talked one way and steadily believed another.

This is where *Major Barbara* steps in, and why it moves so surely and firmly to the heart of the issue. Shaw's play makes its point by the simple expedient of exploiting this unacknowledged commitment of ours. Its dramatic formula is the same as in other Shaw plays. We think we are laughing because it manufactures a paradox, because it turns things upside down and makes the worse cause appear the better cause. But we discover as we proceed that everything follows logically from what we really and seriously believe, that Shaw is speaking our inmost minds.

Major Barbara, in other words, turns on an ultimate dramatic device which is the same as that in Plato's dialogues. It invokes the audience's own deepest convictions, and employs them to upset what the audience thinks it believes or would like to believe. The political thinking in *Major Barbara* is in the tradition of Machiavelli and Hobbes, Nietzsche and Marx. These were not when Shaw wrote, and they are not now, pleasant names to conjure with. They are all "materialists," antimoralists, the great doctrinaires of Power. But *Major Barbara* makes us see that they are all speaking for us, and that we dislike them only because they are telling everybody's secret. And it makes us see that there is no choice between Power and Virtue. There is only an undiscriminating and a discriminating use of power, an unimaginative and an imaginative use, a use for ends that are imposed on us and a use for ends we choose for ourselves freely and responsibly.

Major Barbara offers us a choice, or so it seems, between religion and munitionsmaking, goodness and success, the generous heart and the well filled pocketbook. And in every case it opts for the latter of these alternatives. It tells us that the body is more important than the spirit, that efficiency is better than personal goodness, and, indeed, that conventional goodness is generally only an excuse for inefficiency. It presents us with a choice between the two grand methods of affecting human behavior. The first is the method of regenerating individuals, of appealing to their better natures—the method of the Salvation Army. And it shows us the Salvation Army making its furtive but unavoidable peace with the facts of power: without the whisky industry the Salvation Army could not carry on its struggle against alcoholism for a single day. Everybody, even the most virtuous, is touched by social power and controlled by it; and if this power is immoral, then everybody depends on this immorality and lives on it. And then, on the other side, the play presents us with a second method for affecting human behavior. This is the method of Undershaft, the method of social engineering which does not preach at poverty and weakness, but quite simply kills them.

What bothers us, of course, is not that Shaw says that money and power are what actually count in the world. We all know that, or say that we do. Nor does it bother us too much that Shaw exhibits the disparity between the code of Power we live by and the code of Virtue we profess. We all enjoy being called down for our vices, and we would in fact be much more comfortable if we could take *Major Barbara* simply as an attack on our hypocrisy. What bothers us is that Shaw joyfully turns Power into a moral system and holds everything up to criticism in its light. He does not ask us to be more virtuous, to be more sincere about living up to our professions. He asks us to be more sincere about our actual practice, to take its principles seriously and to see them through to their logical conclusions, to regard poverty and weakness consistently as crimes, and to turn the love of money and power into a moral code. The universal regard for money, he tells us, is the one hopeful fact in our civilization, the one sound spot in our social conscience.

This, of course, is what hurts. For while we may admit that we all love money, we hate to see ourselves glorified for it. It takes all the fun—or should I say the Sin?—out of it. We find ourselves disliking the man who tells us that there is nothing wrong, and everything right, in liking the one thing we obviously do like. And surprisingly, we do not think it consoling or conservative, we think it troubling and revolutionary. Indeed, the man who turns out to be comforting, and really on the side of the *status quo,* is the man who says that we should all change our values and undergo some sort of radical spiritual conversion.

It would be comforting to believe that Shaw is saying all this with his tongue in his cheek. But he is, of course, in deadly earnest. He does not want us to stop loving money and power. He wants us to love money and power seriously and unashamedly, to commit ourselves to them, and to what the love of them entails. What are the reasons for this remarkably straightforward espousal of the morality of Power? The reasons are the classic ones—the reasons of Machiavelli and Hobbes and Marx and Nietzsche. And they show, I think, that Shaw is right.

In the first place, most moral exhortation is majestically, indeed callously, irrelevant. It is irrelevant in the way in which it is irrelevant to tell a man playing football that hard tackling hurts. It is irrelevant because the standards which most moralists employ have almost nothing to do with the choices that men actually have to make. While moralists talk, history goes on behind their backs. For moral talk is relevant only when the individual can be held responsible for his choices, when it is possible for him to do otherwise than he is doing and to meet the standards that the moralist is imposing on him. But very little moral talk is really of this kind. And if it were, it would be rooted in facts and not in *a priori* ideals. It would be a morality of power and not of abstract goodness.

Secondly, most moral exhortation is in the profoundest sense hypocritical. For only the love of power, as Shaw points out, stands the test of the categorical imperative. If everybody acted as Undershaft does, if everybody made it a point of honor to have money and power, if everybody would rather die than be poor and weak, the result would not be horrible at all. The result would be a revolution of incalculable benefice. For it is an obvious and elementary fact that it is not power but weakness that makes men's lives nasty, brutish, mean, and short. "I was a dangerous man," says Undershaft, "until I had my will. Now I am a useful, beneficent, kindly person. When that is the history of every Englishman, we shall have an England worth living in." And as for our alleged love of Virtue, we do not, of course, really want everybody to be virtuous, come hell or high-water. Despite all our talk about the absolute character of morality, our moral judgments are in fact relative and circumstantial. We are all for truth and honor and brotherly love, for example, and we hope that our diplomats will go forth armed with these ideals. But we would complain, and we would have a right to complain, if they negotiated on this basis.

Moral talk, of course, has its functions. In particular, it does two things without which, I suppose, we could not live. It allows us, in the first place, to punish and be punished, to forgive and be forgiven. It allows us to feel, in other words, what we want above all else to feel—that the evil we do is revocable, that we can take it back or give it back. And it is very important to be allowed to feel this way, because it permits us to go on doing what we have been doing. Bill Walker, who punches Jenny Hill in the jaw, wants only to be punched in return. Failing that, he would like to pay his pound and be even. He wants to have his moral accounts balanced. The one thing that does not occur to him is that he might stop punching young ladies in the jaw.

In the second place, moral preaching satisfies something it ostensibly opposes—namely, our love of power. This is the great secret weapon of the preacher. Hypocrisy, some one has said, is the tribute vice pays to virtue; well, moral talk is the poor man's substitute for power. Next to really having power, talk about Virtue is unbeatable as a way of building up a man's ego. This is true even when we flay that ego. For it makes the individual feel that he can change the world just by changing himself, that his struggle with his own soul is the struggle that will settle the destiny of mankind. Nothing could be more consoling. "My dear: you are the incarnation of morality," Undershaft says to his wife. "Your conscience is clear and your duty done when you have called everybody names."

But moral exhortation serves these convenient purposes at a fearful price. Psychologically, it puts an extra, and unnecessarily cruel, burden of anxiety on people. Sociologically, it systematically misleads them, for the great trouble with most preaching is that it diagnoses the source of the trouble wrongly. It talks about walking upright, when the rooms in which men walk have low ceilings. It talks about individual regeneration, when the trouble is the social paths that are open. It substitutes, in a word, anxiety for action, and empty and indignant words for a political program. It seems to me, therefore, that Machiavelli and Hobbes and Nietzsche and Shaw are right. Conventional morality is generally the snare of the weak and the consolation of the powerless. And I say this seriously, and I hope soberly.

Yet it is impossible, of course, to be quite happy with this conclusion, for it is plain that this very criticism of conventional morality rests on certain moral ideals. And there is a great deal more in *Major Barbara* itself to suggest that this is not all that Shaw has to say on the subject.

To begin with, Major Barbara herself has Virtue. It is not a conventional kind of virtue, but it is a very rare kind of power. It reduces bullies to helplessness, it makes men fall in love with her and gives them a purpose in life they had never had before. And then it is not Undershaft who gets his way in the end. It is the professor of Greek, the heir to the subtlest poetry and philosophy the Western mind has produced, the man who bears the name of the most tragic and radical of the Greek playwrights. The professor of Greek gets the girl, he gets the factory, he gets the right of way. And he tells Undershaft that he will not sell the instruments of death—and, consequently, of life—indiscriminately, as Undershaft has done. He will sell them only to whom he pleases, for he sees that Undershaft really has no power of his own, that he does not own his business, that his business owns him.

For this is the rub. Power can come full circle on those who possess it and make them its slaves. If we go back in the history of thought, we find that those who have been the most unflinching doctrinaires of Power have not been men without ideals. They have been men with some one absolute ideal which shunted everything else aside. For Hobbes it was peace, for Machiavelli the unification of Italy, for Lenin socialism. And this is why they could make a cult of Power. They made a cult of Power because they had already made an irrevocable decision as to what Power was for, and had stopped worrying about it. They are, in fact, in precisely the same position as those who have made a cult of abstract Virtue. For if we turn back and look at those who, like Plato or Rousseau, have been the most unflinching partisans of Virtue, and have singlemindedly worshipped some one ideal at the expense of all others, we find that they, too, are prepared to endorse any and every means that seems to them to serve this end.

The partisans of Goodness in the abstract, in other words, are the blood brothers of the partisans of Power in the abstract. The cult of Power and the cult of Virtue are only the two sides of the same coin —and the coin is a commitment to a moral absolute, a devotion to some one objective in the conviction that it takes care of everything else.

In short, we do not have to make the choice between Efficient Power and Inefficient Virtue. This is only one more of the lingering confusions our hereditary intellectual absolutism has visited upon us. We can avoid both horns of the dilemma the moment we take a relativistic and provisional view of human ideals. For if we see that the goal we are seeking is not necessarily the only goal there is, we will not normally want to commit all our power to it. We will want to keep some power in reserve, we will want to see that it is not too heavily concentrated behind some one set of interests, we will want to erect safeguards. We will want, that is, not to moralize Power into something else, but to control what any one man can do with it by seeing that others have power, too. The problem of Power, in a word, becomes the problem of distributing it, not of eliminating it.

And if we take a relativistic view, we see something else, too— the role of ideals. For if there is more than one purpose that men may legitimately seek, we have to be able to choose among them. We need ideals—not to make Power "moral" but simply to know how and for what purpose to use it. "I want to make power for the world," says Major Barbara, "but it must be spiritual power." "I think all power is spiritual," her lover answers. "These cannons will not go off by themselves." As a distinguished teacher once told me, the sad history of our civilization can be told in the decline of the word "Virtue": it began among the Greeks by meaning strength in a man and it ended among the Victorians by meaning weakness in a woman. It would be a help to intellectual clarity if we did not think of Virtue as something external to Power, as something feminine which comes down like an angel and saves Power from its inherent male coarseness, and thought of it instead in its primal sense as standing for strength or skill. So understood, Virtue is not an alternative to Power. It is the skillful use of Power for freely chosen ends. Virtue without Power is empty; but Power without Virtue, without ideas, is blind.

In short, it is only the worship of absolutes that leads us to the impasse of having to choose between being inefficient and being good; but if we must do without absolutes, this does not mean that we can get along without having any vision at all. We do not have to agree with everything in Shaw—with his own program for social reform, for example, or with his contempt for parliamentary routines, or with his deeplying admiration for "strong men." But *Major Barbara* can teach us a number of things. It can teach us that the choice is not between Efficient Power and Inefficient Virtue, but between using our powers blindly and using them for ends we deliberately select. It can teach us that there is a difference between prating about Virtue and soberly setting out to do what the facts of Power permit. It can teach us that political reform does not follow from moral regeneration nearly so much as moral regeneration follows from social reform. It can teach us that Power is not something inherently immoral, and that, like money, it is only when it is cheapened to worthlessness for some and made impossibly dear to others, that it becomes a curse.

And *Major Barbara* can remind us finally of what we seem to have forgotten—what it means to think politically. For Shaw does two things in this play—he looks the facts of Power coolly in the face, and he sees a light shining through them. It was not their respect for Power that led Machiavelli or Hobbes or Marx to make a fetish of it. It was their self-blinding devotion to a single absolute ideal at the expense of everything else. But what lifted these men above the level of opportunists and political hacks is the simple fact that they had a vision of something beyond Power. This is why their realism strikes fire and their love of Power was contagious. It was a borrowed contagion. We should remember that it is not Undershaft the moneybags who makes his point in *Major Barbara*. It is Undershaft the visionary, the man for whom being a millionaire is a religion—a mystic who is the conscious bearer of a Power that does not belong to him, and the conscious servant of ends not his own. The task is to formulate these ends explicitly, in the light of what our existing powers make possible, and to seek them deliberately. The false dilemma of Power *versus* Virtue merely keeps us from getting ahead with this job.

III

ART AT WAR WITH THE GOOD

(Thomas Mann: *Death in Venice*)

BY

GEORGE N. SHUSTER

Miss Edna St. Vincent Millay's line, "Euclid alone has looked on Beauty bare," leads by a somewhat circuitous route to the theme and symbols of Thomas Mann's *Der Tod in Venedig*. For was not the problem which Gustav Aschenbach failed to solve, as he apparently had so many others compounded of morality and art, this—how "heroically" to

> seek release
> From dusty bondage into luminous air?

The bondage was in his case that of high art, served with ascetic fidelity. For its sake he had not merely set himself apart from the world—a divorce which in Mann's earlier work is considered inevitable and fateful—but had steeled his will to pay unflagging homage to the fragment of vision or insight which waited every morning to be caught in words. No monk could have gone to his hour of contemplative prayer more reverently than Aschenbach did to his time of closeting with a Muse who lifted him as the years passed above everything that might have made the slavery petty or indolent. And then a sudden, tragic, even sordid involvement from which he was powerless to extricate himself, which was derived from meditative awareness of a beauty he was unable to master or absorb! Here was the flame in which he, unbelievably turned moth, must die; and in this demise there were implicit both the irony of his unfulfilment and the tragedy of his self-repudiation.

Der Tod in Venedig, in many ways the most effectively written and yet the least typical of Mann's shorter stories, was finished in 1911, that is, at a time when it was still possible to visualize tragedy in the dimensions of the individual rather than of humanity; and yet the fable retains a universal cultural significance not less striking than that of Kafka's *Castle,* though to be sure the underlying assumptions are quite different. The author's later allusions to it are shy, as if he were troubled by this child of his art. Commenting in *Betrachtungen eines Unpolitischen* on the fact that through him, "as through every other relatively sensitive instrument," the shape of things to come was indicated, he says: "Then too I see clearly how in a way the story *Der Tod in Venedig* is rooted in the time, and that what it tells of straining of the will and of morbidity reflects the imminence of war. It is in its way something final, the last fruit of an era on which the uncertain lights of a newer time play."

Yet one should not assume that this singularity implies the parentage of ideas other than those which then formed Mann's views of life and art. Nietzsche, Schopenhauer, and Wagner are ancestors in this case, too; and no doubt Mann had already then been captivated by the dissonance between Goethe and Schiller, which a reader of English literature might compare to the difference between Dickens and Thackeray, or Shakespeare and Ben Jonson. As the rich, complex but strangely chaotic essay entitled *Goethe und Tolstoi,* published in 1932, makes evident, Mann saw in Goethe a sort of quintessence of ontology incarnate, for whom Nature was mirrored in its humanized fullness in himself, whereas Schiller was mind shaping life to the contours of what ought to be. Aschenbach's categorical imperatives are, however, almost purely esthetic. When he had once lain ill in Vienna, someone had described him, with suggestive pantomime, as a man who had never lived ludicrously or lewdly. And so one may surmise, by way of prelude, that unlike Goethe, whom a voyage to Italy had restored to his full powers, the Schiller emulator Aschenbach would be brought down with a sickening thud as soon as the world of the Mediterranean was revealed to him in its fullness and corruption. There are other haunting overtones of suggestion. It was to Venice that Richard Wagner, driven from the Asyl by a restlessness which would not permit him to get his work done, had come in 1854 to compose the second act of *Tristan*. And it was there that he had also written letters which reflect more than any others the kinship between his moods and those of Schopenhauer. One may also recall that in *Mort de Venise,* Maurice Barres assembled his company of unhappy immortals, merging their quest for beauty in the apprehension of death. It is perhaps noteworthy, that a German writer and a French writer should, at approximately the same time, have found the city of Doges and canals a proper setting for their versions of the Tristan theme. But with this the resemblance ceases. Mann who during the First World War was almost as vigorous a defender of German culture as Barres was its critic, did not find *Mort de Venise* to his liking. And the French book is, to be sure, a manifesto, almost rhetorical in quality, while *Der Tod in Venedig* is a triumph of grim objectivity, though it is not for all that devoid of subjective implications and interests.

The story itself is told in three undemarcated acts, which one may define as the setting, the warning, and the drama. Aschenbach, a famous writer who has even been knighted for a novel about Frederick the Great, is shown as one who has triumphed over the physical debilities which had doomed so many of his lineage to talented unfruition. His own literary powers had been manifest at an early age; and, to quote Mann's words, "after some years of restlessness, and a few attempts to settle down in one place or another, he had relatively early chosen Munich as his permanent residence and dwelt there in a state of civic dignity, such as upon occasion a man of spirit is privileged to enjoy. The marriage he had contracted in his youth with a girl of scholarly family, was dissolved by death after a brief period of happiness. He had a daughter who was already married. A son he never had."

In terms of the German culture of his time, Aschenbach's personal life resembled that of many an army officer who then lived by the maxims of Kant and Moltke, subordinating his personal happiness to the probity of his profession. It is interesting to note that Mann does not describe the houses in which Aschenbach lived. One learns only of the writing table with its brace of candles, and is told that at his little home in the mountains one servant prepared his meals while another served them. But there is a great deal about the discipline to which this man of letters subjected himself. After years of effort he had removed from his writing every commonplace word—his way, no doubt, of observing one of the most memorable of Goethe's maxims; and though he dealt honestly with life problems, which his younger readers considered the only things worth writing about, he was scrupulously addicted to a style of classical purity and to the enunciation of ethical principles of such nobility that passages from his books had been included in school texts. In short, he combined what Frenchmen of approximately the same period were terming *culte de moi* and *l'art pour l'art*. And Thomas Mann, one of the final products of German Romanticism, would not be Mann if he did not inject into this description at the pertinent moment a query as to whether these twin pursuits might not have blinded Aschenbach to the fact that there is latent in service to art a temptation to subordinate morality to the norms of beauty.

From all this absorbing endeavor Aschenbach decides quite irrationally to emancipate himself for a brief spell and to seek in travel some stimulus of the sensations which he, at the turn of middle age, seems to require. There is implicit in this decision some half-conscious hankering after the fountains of youth—a lassitude built into the lifespan—but the need lies deeper, too. Something like a dark night of the spirit has invaded his cell. The soldier has tired of the drill of art. And now there loom up three sentinels of disaster who for many a reader will seem modern replicas of the witches in *Macbeth*. The first is a chance, enigmatic, wholly Bohemian, and strangely alien figure who turns up from nowhere as Aschenbach is strolling through the English Garden, disturbing the writer not by reason of what he is but of what he suggests of far away and unwholesome places. The second is the horrible bawdy, antique homosexual who, with a group of young folk, comes aboard the filthy tramp steamer which takes Aschenbach to Venice from the resort island where he has been bored to the point of extinction. And the third, no doubt the most striking of the three, is the lawless freebooter who by chance is the gondolier who takes Aschenbach to his destination on a vessel suggesting beauty and death. This unlicensed boatman, young and rude, is the un-tamed violator of custom who serves fittingly as the initiator into Venice itself, city which despite the Brownings has, from time im-memorial, symbolized immorality. In his day Roger Ascham in-veighed against it in behalf of English Puritanism; in our own, Frederick Corvo appropriately went to pieces there.

These three heralds are in the great Romantic tradition, which continued the medieval pattern that found its supreme utterance in Shakespeare. They hint at absorbing possibilities. What warnings come out of the darkness in which man moves? Human life is al-ways like a walk taken down an unlighted street by a man with a lantern in his hand. May not unseen things jostle him there, even as unimagined verities strut through his subconscious mind? Over and over again one sees repeated in great literature knocks on the window —frequently three in number—which warn of impending fate. Con-sider Nancy in *Oliver Twist,* or Caesar in the great play which bears his name. Yet if one looks upon all this as literary artifice only, the effect is unmistakable. The *leit-motifs* have been sounded and the drama begins.

There appears the figure of Tadzio, the boy who becomes for Aschenbach the incarnation of exquisite beauty, and of that alone, never to be seized or enjoyed save in the beholding, this proximate enough to be morally perilous and yet forever so remote that there is no bridge from it to life. I have said "the figure of Tadzio" because what is revealed of him is only silhouette. That Aschenbach's in-fatuation is pederastic is, however, of the greatest significance. The boy called to mind "Greek sculpture of the noblest period," while his three sisters were dressed with such crudity and chasteness that their faces and figures were actually distorted. This contrast between normal and abnormal is brought into even sharper relief by the little one actually learns about Tadzio as a person. He is a graceful, golden haired, somewhat fragile boy with the profile of a young god, who walks on the sand or swims in the water, who saunters into the dining room and looks casually about him, whose relationships with other young people are not intimate though they may be friendly. Mann said later on that Tadzio was conceived of as *notwendig liederlich,* which one may translate as by innate compulsion awakening and coveting in return sexual desire. But surely what Aschenbach sees of him is merely amoral, in some primitive but still classical way pagan. He cannot approach the boy because to do so would mean running afoul of the law and of social custom. But he also cannot shut out the wish to see him, to reinforce with his physical presence the dream's impact. It is the plague which then dungs Venice with death that ushers in the somber, somehow demonical finale. A voyage entered upon the quest for a new accession of youth ends instead with an appalling accentuation of old age. Aschenbach sits calmly while a Venetian barber powders and paints his face and dyes his hair into a semblance of that of early manhood. Then, deepest degradation of all, his spirit succumbs to perverse desire. He garbles a noble text of Plato so as to make Socrates identify the Good with lechery. While the beloved boy cavorts on the beach, the stricken writer dies. His public learns only of his unexpected demise in a far away country.

What is perhaps most striking about the quality of this drama is that it enkindles no tragic emotion. One is removed as far as may well be possible from the *catharsis* which was the noble concern of Greek dramatic art to witness an almost clinical dissection of an obsession—something, though it be only that, the book has in common with Henry James' *Turn of the Screw*. It is quite as if the warnings had been no more than symptoms akin to the hemorrhages which indicate the presence of a duodenal ulcer. Aschenbach's infatuation was the product of his way of life. But the determinism which thus underlies the narrative should not, I think, be understood in a Freudian sense. Aschenbach's abstentions do not affect the outcome in any genuinely effective way, though they may perhaps be conditions which accelerate the progress of the disease. The cause is rather an infection present in the European dedication to high art as that through the cultivation of which man can achieve the highest form of living. In this sense the book is at once a child of Nietzsche and a critique of his views. It says in fact—or appears to say, at least—that giving oneself up to an ideate of life which requires the putting aside of life itself can only lead to death. And indeed the corrosion and demise of the spirit thus achieved is more terrifying than others, because the poison which can be distilled from beauty is an agent of decomposition more effective than any comparable venom.

This idea, which as is well known has haunted Thomas Mann all his days and has sometimes led him to curious experiments with esthetic and moral doctrine, is of course based in part on the quite normal abnormality of the spiritual life, whether it be artistic, intellectual, or religious. It is the sense of being shunted off the main street of life which drove Faust into that street in the hope of discovering the treasure he had not possessed. And of course the same variety of dubiousness and inquiry finds expression, in a different manner, in Mann's *Tonio Kroeger*. Yes, on another level it was Tolstoy's unwillingness to sacrifice his immense vitality to any cause which did not provide room for all of it, for animal cavorting, neighborly patting on the back, and forgathering in Christian prayer, which impelled him to so many vehement outbursts of emotional expression and commitment. Yet there are things about Gustav Aschenbach which are not to be explained in this wise, and no doubt it is on them that attention must be focused.

Paul Bourget, the French novelist whose *Essais de psychologie contemporaire* continue to afford much insight into the state of the European mind prior to the First World War, wrote a novel which in some respects resembles *Tod in Venedig*. This is entitled *Le Demon du Midi,* based on a biblical text warning of the perils of the noonday of life. The hero, a middle-aged Catholic church historian of hitherto irreproachable morals, enters into an adulterous liaison with a woman of great charm but, to say the least, of considerable competence in the area of sin. The resultant shattering of the hero's life constituted what Bourget was wont to call a *roman à these*—that is, a novel which presumably demonstrated that the consequences of sexual passion, particularly if indulged by church historians, are horrifying enough to deter even the most amorous, granted a modicum of sage reflection. Thus stated, of course, the theme of the novel is not convincing. But it is a much better book than the thesis would suggest. Bourget was deeply persuaded that modern man suffered from what he called "a malady of the will." The desire for fame or success led to all sorts of compromises with inner integrity. And his novel is therefore a tragedy of the decomposition of the will under the stress of temptation which one reads with a feeling that it is a tragedy, and of the hero of which one says, "There but for the grace of God go I." In short, here is a book written in the tradition of religious culture, in which determinism exists only as a pathological phenomenon, and responsibility is the norm. Had Bourget dealt with Gustav Aschenbach, he would no doubt have tried to show that little by little an erosion of the ethical imperative had taken place, leaving the man naked unto his emotional and moral enemies. This would no doubt have been a valid hypothesis, but for a variety of reasons it is not one which would have occurred to Thomas Mann.

It was, I believe, Kenneth Burke, who first sketched a parallel between *Tod in Venedig* and Andre Gide's *The Immoralist.* The following passage from an essay which bears the title, *The Stature of Thomas Mann,* is pertinent.

Despite the parallelism between *Death in Venice* and *The Immoralist,* the emphasis is very different. Whereas in Mann we feel most the sense of resistance, of resignation to the point of distress, and Aschenbach's dissolution is matched by a constant straining after self-discipline, in Gide we hear a narrator who relates with more than pride, with something akin to positive advocacy, the unclean details of his life. *"Je vais vous parler longuement de mon corps,"* he opens one chapter in a tone which I sometimes regret he has seen fit to drop from his later work; there is no mistaking its connotations; it is the accent of evangelism, of pleading.

Burke goes on to say that Gide's novels, dissolute though they may appear to be, are really essays on the subject of the Divine pursuit of each individual soul down the labyrinths of good and evil which are of its own choosing, whereas Mann is primarily concerned with the fact that, in his view, man has only the opportunity to express a preference for one of several antinomies which are mutually exclusive. He cannot, for instance, be a lover of both truth and beauty. We may argue, as many have, that the actual influence of Gide is corrosive whereas that of Mann is not. But I think there can be no doubt that whereas the great Frenchman was haunted by the ever repeated drama of redemption, the German has not been.

And so we are left finally with some necessity for reflecting on whether there is in our lives some such dichotomy between the beautiful and the good as Mann projects. It is as if we were asked to write a gloss on the story of Eve and the apple which was offered to her by the serpent in Paradise. Assuming that God is "Beauty bare," and that the apple is loveliness in all its reflected forms, of the flesh and otherwise, is there any way of reconciling the two? Or, in other words, must we conclude that the reflections are lures leading away from the reality? The evidence in favor of an affirmative response is surely very impressive. St. Augustine, in *De Musica* especially, echoed the strictures which had been expressed by Plato against all the endeavors of the poets. "If thine eye offend thee, pluck it out," says the New Testament. Yet there is very much to be said for the negative as well. The same New Testament assures its readers that if they seek first the Kingdom of God, all the other things will be given to them.

One must, however, attempt to formulate the problem in Mann's terms which are not those of Judeo-Christian asceticism but rather those of the foremost German Romantics. In the *Ich-Kosmos* reality as apprehended by the artist or the thinker is always of necessity a coming together of things that do not belong together. Just as the figure of St. Sebastian is eventually nothing but a quivering victim in whom many spears are lodged, so also the Romantic *Ich* develops into an organic weaving together of contradictory and complementary insights, the synthesis of which is a product not of analysis but of concrete apprehension—of what, for lack of any other appropriate word, one may call *Wesensschau*. That this apprehension is necessarily painful will be clear to anyone who tries to think of life and death at the same time. And so quite logically the best new books about Goethe sketch the portrait of a sufferer, of an unremittingly self-exhausting wrestler, rather than of a serene Olympian. Such suffering and wrestling can go on, however, only if there is a source of strength sufficiently noble and austere. For the young Mann, as for many others, this source had been indicated by Friedrich Nietzsche and Arthur Schopenhauer; and to what they said one could add the testimony of the great Russians. In *Betrachtungen eines Unpolitischen* there is cited with great force this passage from the close of Tolstoy's *Lucerne:*

What an unhappy, miserable creature man is then, who despite his thirst for positive solutions, is cast into this eternally heaving, shoreless sea of good and evil, of facts, considerations and contradictions! If only human beings had learned finally not to judge and think so sharply, uncompromisingly, and not to be giving perpetually answers to questions which have only been presented so that they may always remain questions. If only they would remember that every idea is at the same time false and true. It is false because man is prejudiced and cannot possibly comprehend truth in its fullness. It is true because in it always one side of human aspiration is reflected. Acting in this turbulent, shoreless, infinitely eddying chaos of good and evil men have created bodies of knowledge and thought, they have marked out imaginary boundary lines in this sea; and so they expect that the waters will respect those lines of demarcation. As if there were not millions of other partitions made on the basis of wholly different considerations. . . . We say that civilization is good and the primitive bad; that freedom is good, and lack of freedom evil. This illusory knowledge destroys in human nature the instinctive, holy, aboriginal quest for the Good. Who can tell us what freedom is, what despotism, what civilization and what barbarism? . . . Infinite is the goodness and wisdom of him who permits these contradictions to exist and has indeed ordained them. Only you, miserable worm, who impudently and brazenly seeks to fathom his laws and his counsels, conceive of them as contradictions. He looks gently down from his luminous unapproachable high place and is pleased with the unending harmony in which all of you move in eternal contradiction.

What are associated in this passage are of course cultural pessimism and profound faith. But if one reads honestly one can find no such weaving together of humility and resignation in *Tod in Venedig*. What happens is that the *Ich-Kosmos* of Gustav Aschenbach is invaded by a force it cannot repel because it cannot see the thing clearly. Once again the ruse of the Trojan Horse has succeeded. Beauty is the recipe for death because beauty is always simulating or concealing death. The pages in which the first shock of the entry are described combine psychological subtlety with a quite extraordinary mastery of expression. Aschenbach, finding the weather not to his liking (he is almost as sensitive to atmospheric changes as Nietzsche was) seriously considers leaving Venice. But as he sits eating and trying to make up his mind, the boy enters the dining salon—with "the head of Eros, of the yellowish texture of Parian marble." Aschenbach, we read, acknowledged the presence of Tadzio "with that cool professional approval in which artists now and then clothe their ecstasy, their sense of overpowering joy, in the presence of a masterpiece." Therewith he combines the fateful decision to remain; and in the days that follow boy and sea and beach merge into a unity which absorbs the creative personality of Aschenbach wholly, relentlessly. That the experience should be blended always with banality—that of the boy's own going and coming, and that of the life on the beach—is of the very essence of the grim irony of the tale. The quest for the beautiful has led to its own contradiction. The master has become the slave. He who stood above all the battles of life, is now the merest private in the ranks.

If one asks how the invasion could have been halted, no answer is forthcoming. It may be argued that none should be expected—that a novelist's business is to tell his story and the rest be damned; and I shall concede that in this instance there would have been esthetic challenge enough. Yet it may also be true that a secret about the *Ich-Kosmos* has slipped out. Perhaps the asceticism implicit in baring the ego to all the manifold images in which the contradictions of existence are subjected to the reign of creative personality, may involve not being able to keep out the one which will be destructive. This is a little like welcoming scientists to Los Alamos or Brookhaven while not being certain that a traitorous one will not undo the purpose of the whole enterprise. Nietzsche, with his cult of suffering for mankind all its indignities, eventually concluded that he was the Messiah. And Aschenbach was deluded into thinking that he might be the possessor rather than the servant of art.

There is finally another way of looking at this episode in the life of an unfortunate man. May Aschenbach's fate not be the result of giving in to an illusion that an escape from his serfdom was possible? May it be that the artist building an *Ich-Kosmos* is recruited for his own excruciating if rewarding form of helotry, and that therefore escapism is for him a gross and grave revolt, the consequence of which can only be death? Such queries are not likely to seem as real now as they undoubtedly were during the early years of the century. But they are nevertheless always with us. I have sometimes fancied that the relationship between Romanticism, as it expresses itself in Thomas Mann, and Judeo-Christianity, is very nearly like that which De Witt assumes once existed between the Epicurean philosophers and St. Paul. For Mann escapism consists not in an attempt to evade the pursuit of the Divine Eros—one recalls Augustine's *cor nostrum inquietum est donec requiet in te*—but in the effort to fancy that the esthetic imperative can be put in the closet while the artist goes for a walk. The basic difference is that from the first there is Redemption. From the second there is none.

IV

THE MORALITY OF INERTIA

(Edith Wharton: *Ethan Frome*)

LIONEL TRILLING

When The Institute for Religious and Social Studies of The Jewish
Theological Seminary of America planned a series of lectures on
"Literary Presentations of Great Moral Issues" and asked me to give
one of the talks, I was disposed to accept the invitation, for I have a
weakness for the general subject. But I hesitated over the particular
instance, for I was asked to discuss the moral issues in *Ethan Frome*. I
had not read Edith Wharton's little novel in a good many years, but
I remembered it with no pleasure or admiration. I recalled it as not
at all the sort of book that deserved to stand in a list which included
The Brothers Karamazov and *Billy Budd, Foretopman*. If it presented a moral issue at all, I could not bring to mind what that issue
was. And so I postponed my acceptance of the invitation and made it
conditional upon my being able to come to terms with the subject
assigned to me.

Ethan Frome, when I read it again, turned out to be pretty much
as I had recalled it. It isn't a great book, or even a fine book. It seemed
to me a factitious book, perhaps even a cruel book. I was puzzled to
understand how it ever came to be put on the list, why anyone should
want to have it discussed as an example of moral perception. Then I
remembered its reputation, which, in America, is very considerable.
It is sometimes spoken of as an American classic. Every literate person
has read it. It is often assigned to high school and college students as
a text for study.

But the high and solemn repute in which it stands is, I am sure, in large part a mere accident of American culture. *Ethan Frome* appeared in 1911, at a time when, to a degree that we can now only wonder at, American literature was committed to optimism, cheerfulness, and gentility. What William Dean Howells called "the smiling aspects of life" had an importance in the literature of America some fifty years ago which is unmatched in the literature of any other time and place. It was inevitable that those who were critical of the prevailing culture and who wished to foster in America a higher and more serious literature should put a heavy stress upon the grimmer aspects of life, that they should equate the smiling aspects with falsehood, the grimmer aspects with truth. For these devoted people, sickened as they were by cheerfulness and hope, the word "stark" seemed to carry the highest possible praise a critical review or a blurb could bestow, with "relentless" and "inevitable" as its proper variants. *Ethan Frome* was admired because it was stark—its action, we note, takes place in the New England village of Starkville—and because the fate it describes is *relentless* and *inevitable*.

No one would wish to question any high valuation that may be given to the literary representation of unhappy events—except, perhaps, as the high valuation may be a mere cliché of an intellectual class, except as it is supposed to seem the hallmark of the superior sensibility and intelligence of that class. Then we have the right, and the duty, to look sniffishly at starkness, and relentlessness and inevitability, to cock a skeptical eye at grimness. And I am quite unable to overcome my belief that *Ethan Frome* enjoys its high reputation because it satisfies the modern snobbishness about tragedy and pain.

We can never speak of Edith Wharton without some degree of respect. She brought to her novels a strong if limited intelligence, and notable powers of observation, and a genuine desire to tell the truth, a desire which in some parts she satisfied. But she was a woman in whom we cannot fail to see a limitation of heart, and this limitation makes itself manifest as a literary and moral deficiency of her work, and of *Ethan Frome* especially. It appears in the deadness of her prose, and more flagrantly in the suffering of her characters. When the characters of a story suffer, they do so at the behest of their author—the author is responsible for their suffering and must justify his cruelty by the seriousness of his moral intention. The author of *Ethan Frome,* it seemed to me, could not lay claim to any such justification. Her intention in writing the story was not adequate to the dreadful fate she contrives for her characters. She but indulges herself by what she contrives—she is, as the phrase goes, "merely literary." This is not to say that the merely literary intention does not make its very considerable effects. There is in *Ethan Frome* an image of life-in-death, of hell-on-earth, which is not easily to be forgotten: the crippled Ethan, and Zeena, his dreadful wife, and Mattie, the once charming girl he had loved, now bedridden and querulous with pain, all living out their death in the kitchen of the desolate Frome farm—a perpetuity of suffering memorializes a moment of passion. It is terrible to contemplate, it is unforgettable, but the mind can do nothing with it, can only endure it.

My new reading of the book, then, did not lead me to suppose that it justified its reputation, but only confirmed my recollection that *Ethan Frome* was a dead book, the product of mere will, of the cold hard literary will. What is more, it seemed to me quite unavailable to any moral discourse. In the context of morality, there is nothing to say about *Ethan Frome.* It presents no moral issue at all.

For consider the story it tells. A young man of good and gentle character is the only son of a New England farm couple. He has some intellectual gifts and some desire to know the world, and for a year he is happy attending a technical school in a nearby city. But his father is incapacitated by a farm accident, and Ethan dutifully returns to manage the failing farm and sawmill. His father dies; his mother loses her mental faculties, and during her last illness she is nursed by a female relative whom young Ethan marries, for no reason other than that he is bemused by loneliness. The new wife immediately becomes a shrew, a harridan, and a valetudinarian—she lives only to be ill. Because Zeena now must spare herself, the Fromes take into their home a gentle and charming young girl, a destitute cousin of the wife. Ethan and Mattie fall in love, innocently but deeply. The wife, perceiving this, plans to send the girl away, her place to be taken by a hired servant whose wages the husband cannot possibly afford. In despair at their separation Mattie and Ethan attempt suicide. They mean to die by sledding down a steep hill and crashing into a great elm at the bottom. Their plan fails: both survive the crash, Ethan to be sorely crippled, Mattie to be bedridden in perpetual pain. Now the wife Zeena surrenders her claim to a mysterious pathology and becomes the devoted nurse and jailer of the lovers. The terrible tableau to which I have referred is ready for our inspection.

It seemed to me that it was quite impossible to talk about this story. This is not to say that the story is without interest as a story, but what interest it may have does not yield discourse, or at least not moral discourse.

But as I began to explain why I could not accept the invitation to lecture about the book, it suddenly came over me how very strange a phenomenon the book made—how remarkable it was that a story should place before us the dreadful image of three ruined and tortured lives, showing how their ruin came about, and yet propose no moral issue of any kind. And if *issue* seems to imply something more precisely formulated than we have a right to demand of a story, then it seemed to me no less remarkable that the book had scarcely any moral reverberation, that strange and often beautiful sound we seem to hear generated in the air by a tale of suffering, a sound which is not always music, which does not always have a "meaning," but which yet entrances us, like the random notes of an Aeolian harp, or merely the sound of the wind in the chimney. The moral sound that *Ethan Frome* makes is a dull thud. And this seemed to me so remarkable, indeed, that, in the very act of saying why I could not possibly discuss *Ethan Frome,* I found the reason why it must be discussed.

It is, as I have suggested, a very great fault in *Ethan Frome* that it presents no moral issue, and no moral reverberation. A certain propriety controls the literary representation of human suffering. This propriety dictates that the representation of pain may not be, as it were, gratuitous; it must not be an end in itself. The naked act of representing, or contemplating, human suffering is a self-indulgence, and it may be a cruelty. Between a tragedy and a spectacle in the

Roman circus there is at least this much similarity, that the pleasure both afford derives from observing the pain of others. A tragedy is always on the verge of cruelty. What saves it from the actuality of cruelty is that it has an intention beyond itself. This intention may be so simple a one as that of getting us to do something practical about the cause of the suffering or to help actual sufferers, or at least to feel that we should; or it may lead us to look beyond apparent causes to those which the author wishes us to think of as more real, such as Fate, or the will of the gods, or the will of God; or it may challenge our fortitude or intelligence or piety.

A sense of the necessity of some such intention animates all considerations of the strange paradox of tragedy. Aristotle is concerned to solve the riddle of how the contemplation of human suffering can possibly be pleasurable, of why its pleasure is permissible. He wanted to know what literary conditions were needed to keep a tragedy from being a mere display of horror. Here it is well to remember that the Greeks were not so concerned as we have been led to believe to keep all dreadful things off the stage—in the presentation of Aristotle's favorite tragedy, the audience saw Jocasta hanging from a beam, it saw the representation of Oedipus's bloody sightless eyesockets. And so Aristotle discovered, or pretended to discover, that tragedy did certain things to protect itself from being merely cruel. It chose, Aristotle said, a certain kind of hero; he was of a certain social and moral stature; he had a certain degree of possibility of free choice, or at least the appearance or illusion of free choice; he must justify his fate, or seem to justify it, by his moral condition, being neither wholly good nor wholly bad, having a particular fault that collaborates with destiny to bring about his ruin. The purpose of all these specifications for the tragic hero is to assure us that we witness something more than mere passivity when we witness the hero's suffering, that we witness something more than suffering, that the suffering has, as we say, some meaning, some show of rationality.

Aristotle's theory of tragedy has had its way with the world to an extent which is perhaps out of proportion to its comprehensiveness and accuracy. Its success is largely due to its having dealt so openly with the paradox of tragedy. It serves to explain away any guilty feelings that we may have at deriving pleasure from suffering.

But at the same time that the world has accepted Aristotle's theory of tragedy, it has also been a little uneasy about some of its implications. The element of the theory that causes uneasiness in modern times is the matter of the stature of the hero. To a society touched by egalitarian sentiments, the requirement that the hero be a man of rank seems to deny the presumed dignity of tragedy to men of lesser status. And to a culture which questions the freedom of the will, Aristotle's hero seems to be a little beside the point. Aristotle's prescription for the tragic hero is clearly connected with his definition, in his *Ethics,* of the nature of an ethical action. He tells us that a truly ethical action must be a free choice between two alternatives. This definition is then wonderfully complicated by a further requirement—that the moral man must be so trained in making the right choice that he makes it as a matter of habit, makes it, as it were, instinctively. Yet it *is* a choice, and reason plays a part in its making. But we, of course, don't give to reason the same place in the moral life that Aristotle gave it. And in general, over the past hundred and fifty years, dramatists and novelists have tried their hand at the representation of human suffering without the particular safeguards against cruelty which Aristotle perceived, or contrived. A very large part of the literature of Western Europe may be understood in terms of an attempt to invert or criticize the heroic prescription of the hero, by burlesque and comedy, or by the insistence on the commonplace, the lowering of the hero's social status and the diminution of his power of reasoned choice. The work of Fielding may serve as a sufficient example of how the mind of Europe has been haunted by the great images and great prescriptions of classical tragedy, and how it has tried to lay that famous ghost. When Fielding calls his hero Tom Jones, he means that his young man is not Orestes or Achilles; when he calls him a foundling, he is suggesting that Tom Jones is not, all appearances to the contrary notwithstanding, Oedipus.

Edith Wharton was following where others led. Her impulse in conceiving the story of Ethan Frome was not, however, that of moral experimentation. It was, as I have said, a purely literary impulse, in the bad sense of the word literary. Her aim is not that of Wordsworth in any of his stories of the suffering poor, to require it of us that we open our minds to realization of the kinds of people whom suffering touches. Nor is it that of Flaubert in *Madame Bovary,* to wring from sordid circumstances all the pity and terror of an ancient tragic fable. Nor is it that of Dickens or Zola, to shake us with the perception of social injustice, to instruct us in the true nature of social life and to dispose us to indignant opinion and action. These are not essentially literary intentions; they are moral intentions. But all that Edith Wharton has in mind is to achieve that grim tableau of which I have spoken, of pain and imprisonment, of life-in-death. About the events that lead up to this tableau, there is nothing she finds to say, nothing whatever. The best we can say about the meaning of the story is that it might perhaps be a subject of discourse in the context of rural sociology—it might be understood to exemplify the thesis that love and joy do not flourish on povertystricken New England farms. If we try to bring it into the context of morality, its meaning is limited to mere cultural considerations—that is, to people who like their literature to show the "smiling aspects of life," it may be thought to say, "This is the aspect that life really has, as grim as this"; while to people who repudiate a literature that represents only the smiling aspects of life it says, "How intelligent and how brave you are to be able to understand that life is as grim as this." It is really not very much to say.

And yet there is in *Ethan Frome* an idea of very considerable importance. It is there by reason of the author's deficiencies, not by reason of her powers—it is there because it suits Edith Wharton's rather dull literary intention to be content with telling a story about people who do not make moral decisions, whose fate cannot have moral reverberations. The idea is this: that moral inertia, the *not* making of moral decisions, constitutes a very large part of the moral life of humanity.

This isn't an idea that literature likes to deal with. Literature is charmed by energy and dislikes inertia. It characteristically represents morality as positive action. The same is true of the moral philosophy of the West—has been true ever since Aristotle defined a truly moral act by its energy of reason, of choice. A later development of this tendency said that an act was really moral only if it went against the inclination of the person performing the act: the idea was parodied as saying that one could not possibly act morally to one's friends, only to one's enemies.

Yet the dull daily world sees something below this delightful preoccupation of literature and moral philosophy. It is aware of the morality of inertia, and of its function as a social base, as a social cement. It knows that duties are done for no other reason than that they are said to be duties; for no other reason, sometimes, than that the doer has not really been able to conceive of any other course, has, perhaps, been afraid to think of any other course. Hobbes said of the Capitol geese that saved Rome by their cackling that they were the salvation of the city, not because they were they but there. How often the moral act is performed not because we are we but because we are there! This is the morality of habit, or the morality of biology. This is Ethan Frome's morality, simple, unquestioning, passive, even masochistic. His duties as a son are discharged because he is a son; his duties as a husband are discharged because he is a husband. He does nothing because he is a moral man. At one point in his story he is brought to moral crisis—he must choose between his habituated duty to his wife and his duty and inclination to the girl he loves. It is quite impossible for him to deal with the dilemma in the high way that literature and moral philosophy prescribe, by reason and choice. Choice is incompatible with his idea of his existence; he can only elect to die.

Literature, of course, is not wholly indifferent to what I have called the morality of habit and biology, the morality of inertia. But literature, when it deals with this morality, is tempted to qualify its dulness by endowing it with a certain high grace. There is never any real moral choice for the Felicité of Flaubert's story, "A Simple Heart." She is all pious habit of virtue, and of blind, unthinking, unquestioning love. There are, of course, actually such people as Felicité, simple, good, loving—quite stupid in their love, not choosing where to bestow it. We meet such people frequently in literature, in the pages of Balzac, Dickens, Dostoievsky, Joyce, Faulkner, Hemingway.

They are of a quite different order of being from those who try the world with their passion and their reason; they are by way of being saints, of the less complicated kind. They do not really exemplify what I mean by the morality of inertia or of biology. Literature is uncomfortable in the representation of the morality of inertia or of biology, and overcomes its discomfort by representing it with the added grace of that extravagance which we denominate saintliness.

But the morality of inertia is to be found in precise exemplification in one of Wordsworth's poems. Wordsworth is preeminent among the writers who experimented in the representation of new kinds and bases of moral action—he has a genius for imputing moral existence to people who, according to the classical morality, should have no life at all. And he has the coldness to make this imputation without at the same time imputing the special grace and interest of saintliness. The poem I have in mind is ostensibly about a flower, but the transition from the symbol to the human fact is clearly, if awkwardly, made. The flower is a small celandine, and the poet observes that it has not, in the natural way of flowers, folded itself against rough weather:

> But lately, one rough day, this Flower I passed
> And recognized it, though in altered form,
> Now standing as an offering to the blast,
> And buffeted at will by rain and storm.
>
> I stopped, and said with inly-muttered voice,
> It doth not love the shower nor seek the cold;
> This neither is its courage nor its choice,
> But its necessity in being old.

Neither courage nor choice, but necessity: it cannot do otherwise. Yet it acts as if by courage and choice. This is the morality imposed by brute circumstance, by biology, by habit, by the unspoken social demand which we have not the strength to refuse, or, often, to imagine refusing. People are scarcely ever praised for living according to this morality—we do not suppose it to be a morality at all until we see it being broken.

This is morality as it is conceived by the great mass of people in the world. And with this conception of morality goes the almost entire negation of any connection between morality and destiny. A superstitious belief in retribution may play its part in the thought of simple people, but essentially they think of catastrophes as fortuitous, without explanation, without reason. They live in the moral universe of the *Book of Job*. In complex lives, morality does in some part determine destiny; in most lives it does not. Between the moral life of Ethan and Mattie and their terrible fate we cannot make any reasonable connection. Only a moral judgment cruel to the point of insanity could speak of it as anything but accidental.

I have not spoken of the morality of inertia in order to praise it but only in order to recognize it, to suggest that when we keep our minds fixed on what the great invigorating books tell us about the moral life, we obscure the large bulking dull mass of moral fact. Morality is not only the high, torturing, brilliant dilemmas of Ivan Karamazov and Captain Vere. It is also the deeds performed without thought, without choice, perhaps even without love, as Zeena Frome ministers to Ethan and Mattie. The morality of inertia, of the dull, unthinking round of daily duties, may, and often does, yield the immorality of inertia; the example that will most readily occur to us is that of the good simple people, so true to their family responsibilities, who gave no thought to the concentration camps in whose shadow they lived. No: the morality of inertia is not to be praised, but it must be recognized. And Edith Wharton's little novel is not to be praised, but it must be recognized for bringing to our attention what we, and literature, so easily forget.

V

WHEN SHOULD WE NOT TELL THE TRUTH?

(Henrik Ibsen: *The Wild Duck*)

BY

JOHN E. SMITH

I

When should we not tell the truth? Our topic is, like Ibsen's play, both profound and bewildering at the same time. Like all rhetorical questions which serve to introduce a subject for consideration, our question is ambiguous, since it may mean: have we any obligation to reveal the truth to others whether they ask us for our views or not? Or it may mean, are we justified in deliberately distorting the facts, that is, of telling lies, in order to achieve some end which seems to us unobtainable in any other way? And in addition to those two questions there are, I am sure, many other meanings to our basic question.

The two questions I have singled out are by no means the same, for, among other things, failure to reveal what we take to be the truth of a situation is not the same thing as telling a lie. No one of us ever does tell the whole truth. Bertrand Russell expressed the point in an arresting way when he called attention to the fact that when a man takes an oath before he testifies in a law court he promises to tell the *whole* truth, a fact which makes every man a perjurer. Lying, on the other hand, is no merely innocent affair. To lie is not simply to be ignorant of truth or to express it only in part; to lie is to withhold the truth deliberately with the intention of achieving some ulterior goal through the deception.

Moreover, our question is intriguing because it is framed in such a way as already to assume that there are times when we should not tell the truth. In this respect our question is like the question about beating one's wife with which everyone is familiar.

If our main question is, as William James would have said, a "double-barrelled" one, our play, *The Wild Duck,* is no less filled with possibilities and surprises. Fortunately, our chief concern with the play is to see what light its situation, its plot, and its characters can throw upon the moral problems just suggested and others to be set forth in the course of our discussion. We may safely leave to the ingenuity of the literary critics and historians discussion of the artistic features of the work and especially consideration of what Ibsen intended to say, as this may be reconstructed from the study of his life and intellectual development and from the comparison of views expressed in this play with those to be found in plays both before and after *The Wild Duck.*

I propose to divide our discussion into three parts: first, a brief survey of the basic situation and the plot within which it develops; secondly, the drawing of some character sketches, particularly of those main figures who will engage our attention; and, thirdly, a closer look at two moral problems which emerge from the play and in which we are all involved, whether we express them in the way I shall suggest or in some other way.

II

The Wild Duck concerns two senior business partners, Werle and old Ekdal, and the effect which certain events in their lives come to have upon their sons, Gregers Werle and Hialmar Ekdal. Werle, senior, as we are permitted to discover, once involved his partner in a fraud and succeeded in placing the blame upon him, with the result that old Ekdal was sent to prison, bankrupted and ruined for life.

Young Werle, as we are also allowed to discover, knew the truth about his father's conduct at the time but allowed himself to be silenced; it is this early silence in the face of truth which turns out to be one of the most powerful motives behind his fanatic devotion to what he called the "claim of the ideal."

Having ruined his partner, Werle, senior, was not yet done. He proved unfaithful to his wife and took up with Gina, a servant in the household, and when she became pregnant he cleverly married her to Hialmar Ekdal, his old partner's son, whom at the same time he set up in business as a commercial photographer. Hialmar, a man distinguished neither for his intelligence nor his independence, is completely deceived by the whole scheme and he even comes to regard old Werle as something of a benefactor seeking to compensate for his old partner's misfortunes.

The play begins in earnest when the scene opens upon Hialmar, his wife Gina and daughter Hedvig, at home in their combined living quarters and photographer's studio. Old Ekdal, described frequently by his son as a shipwrecked old man, is living out his last years with them, and he exists in a make-believe world to which he tries to give some substance by keeping a few fowl and pigeons in the garret. In this way he imagines that he is still in touch with the wild and living things of the forest, where in the old days he had demonstrated his skill as a hunter and tracker of game.

It is into this domestic situation that Gregers is to come, armed with the truth and spurred on by the claim he believes it to have upon him. But before we introduce this strange young man it is necessary to call attention to the principal piece of symbolism around which so much of the play revolves, the wild duck. Despite the enormous difficulty which usually surrounds most attempts to interpret the symbolic elements in literary works, it is a relief to be able to say that the meaning of the duck is relatively clear. Not only is it clear, but its chief meaning is explained time and again throughout the course of the play. As a matter of fact, it is so clear that not even Hialmar Ekdal should have been in a position to misunderstand it, although it is fairly obvious that its full significance eludes him from the beginning to the end of the play.

In the garret is kept a wild duck which has been wounded by a hunter but saved from the certain death usually suffered by wild ducks under such circumstances by a clever dog trained to dive down and retrieve fallen birds. Wild ducks, we are told, dive down into the reeds and the mire when wounded and destroy themselves, never again to rise to the surface. This wild duck, however, has been saved by a clever dog who had the skill to protect the wounded bird from its own self. To grasp the significance of the duck for the ensuing drama, one must come to understand Gregers Werle casting himself in the role of "clever dog" and bent upon rescuing his friend from falsehood and infidelity. Consider the following dialogue from one scene when Gregers has just heard the story of the duck and decides that such a role in life is for him:

Hialmar: Ha! Ha! If you weren't Gregers Werle, what would you like to be?

Gregers: If I should choose, I should like best to be a clever dog.

Gina: A dog!

Hedvig: Oh, no.

Gregers: Yes, an amazingly clever dog; one that goes to the bottom after wild ducks when they dive and bite themselves fast in tangle and sea-weed, down among the ooze.

Hialmar: Upon my word, now Gregers, I don't in the least know what you're driving at.

By the time young Werle appears he has all but broken with his father and decided to give himself up to what he calls "the claim of the ideal" upon him. He will devote himself, so he thinks, to the communication of the truth, the whole truth and nothing but the truth to his friend Hialmar. He will expose his father as a liar; will reveal Gina as one who could deceive her husband and bring upon Hedvig, the little daughter to whom the duck belongs, all the unhappiness which goes with being unwanted, with being, as her father calls her, "an interloper in his house."

Gregers takes a room in the Ekdal house and completes the group which contains, in addition to those we have met, two other characters, Relling, a doctor, and Molvik, a student of theology. The latter is a sorry figure, having long since exchanged his zeal for the spirit of the Lord for the fruit of the vine, while Relling may be described as a minor character with a major meaning, since he most completely embodies the utter rejection of Gregers's conviction that truth and truth alone is the only valid basis for the good life.

There is little need to follow the plot in detail from this point forward. Gregers, acting in the role of savior and bearer of the truth, takes Hialmar off and acquaints him with all the facts pertaining to his situation, both past and present.

Hialmar's response proves contrary to Werle's expectation and in a very melodramatic way, Hialmar covers himself with hurt pride and wounded vanity which, as one suspects, he secretly enjoys. He denounces his wife and refuses to accept Hedvig as his own. He refers to his daughter as an interloper, as one unwanted and no longer to be acknowledged as his daughter. It is this heedless and thoughtless reaction which leads directly to the tragic or perhaps pathetic conclusion of the play. Again it is Gregers who is the instigator, this time filling Hedvig with the ideal of self-sacrifice. Perhaps, he tells her, if she is willing to demonstrate her devotion to her father, to show him by some heroic action that she is bound to him in life, perhaps then, Gregers suggests, Hialmar will take her to himself again as before. And between them they hit upon the idea of sacrificing Hedvig's prize possession—the wild duck.

The youngster is ready to perform the sacrifice and Gregers is pleased with himself for having arrived at such a happy solution, for in addition to bringing the truth to light he supposes himself responsible for filling the lives of his friends with loyalty and devotion as well. From his vantage point the ideal was about to be realized to the full. Hedvig, honest and devoted as she is, sees more deeply into the situation than all the adults; instead of sacrificing a possession which she treasures very much, she gives up to her father her very life.

III

Let us now turn for a brief look at the three characters most directly and closely connected with the two moral problems I want to raise, Hialmar, Gregers, and Relling. Hialmar has been described as the character who has no character and I think that is an apt description. He is weak and, like a fluid, able to take on whatever form is possessed by the vessel into which he is poured. His expressed aim is to recover the fortune of his family, but he does not face the situation as it actually is. He is content to float along on the surface.

He does not take hold of the problem at hand because he is too filled with self-admiration and self-pity. In his house, for example, one never discusses the dark side of life. He is, unfortunately, not distinguished for his intelligence, and there can be no doubt that this fact has a great deal to do with the tragic character of the play. Hialmar is completely devoid of honest self-consciousness or rather we may say that he has a certain self-awareness, but the self of which he is aware is not the one which he actually possesses. Like so many people he does not know who he is. Furthermore, he has little or no comprehension of what Gregers is talking about when he constantly refers to the claim of the ideal, and as a matter of comic relief, some of the most amusing, even if tragic, parts of the play are the scenes in which Gregers, who is himself none too clear as to the meaning of what he is saying, tries to prepare Hialmar for the truth which he is later to divulge. In a sense, Hialmar, of all people in the play, is the one who is least fitted to hear the truth as well as to bear it once it has become plain.

Gregers, in marked contrast to Hialmar, has been described as the idealist who wants to set everything right. He wants to play, following the symbolism of the duck, the role of clever dog, and he sincerely hopes to rescue his friend from being destroyed. His idealism is, however, by no means unmixed. On the one hand, it is sincere, even if naive, for his own experience has led him to reject fraud and deception and he cannot believe that life is impossible without them. On the other hand, his idealism is too clearly a product of his own bad conscience. He is driven by the memory of his former silence; he cannot now put from his mind the fact that he knew the truth about his father but remained silent. The tragedy of the play consists in the fact that although he tells the truth in accordance with his own ideal, the costs which result are not paid by him.

Perhaps Gregers's most striking failure is his ability to remain completely oblivious to the problem of the *means* to be employed in dealing with a delicate situation. He thinks that simply *telling* the truth, blurting it out as it were, is itself a means of putting falsehood to flight. He has not the faintest idea of the possibility that there might be more than one way in which the truth can be brought to bear in a concrete situation. Moreover, he does not betray any awareness whatsoever of the possibility that truth about personal life can be effective only when the persons involved come to know it and to acknowledge it themselves. George Bernard Shaw in his instructive, even if irritating, book *The Quintessence of Ibsenism,* took this point to be the entire essence of the play. The tragedy, he maintained, is that the busybody—Werle—finds out that people cannot be freed from their own failings from without. They must free themselves.

Moreover, Werle does not understand the moral problem involved in his cavalier use of other lives as material for the realization of his own moral self. His main concern is to act in accordance with his own newly found faith and there can be no doubt that he believes himself righteous in telling Hialmar the truth, simply because of his good intention. It is for this reason that he does not stop to consider the matter of consequences; from his perspective the situation can become only what his intention says that it should become. And even after he tells the truth and is confronted with the disastrous effect, he still is not impelled to reflect upon the difficult problem of how to transform a situation based on a lie into one based upon the truth. The only means he can conceive is simply to blurt out the truth and he supposes that this action will of itself set the situation right.

The third character, the one I have called the minor character with the major meaning, is Relling the doctor. He is as realistic and even cynical as the others are naive. He not only claims to have seen the truth, but to have seen right through the truth. He claims to know the truth not only about the particular situation presented in the play, but about the human situation itself and the truth which he proclaims is that life without a life-lie to support it is impossible. His mission may be described as the opposite of Gregers's: Gregers aims to tell the truth regardless of the consequences; Relling is engaged in commending falsehood as the only way to make life bearable. Relling, for example, succeeds in convincing his roommate, Molvik, that he has a demon and that he is demonic, that his drunkenness is not his own fault, that it does not really proceed from himself but proceeds instead from the demonic character, and he finally drives Molvik to the place where he can get as drunk as possible without feeling any responsibility whatever.

On another occasion Relling engages young Ekdal in conversation and convinces him that he ought to pursue work on an invention of value in the business of photography and in that way help to redeem the family fortune. Hialmar himself would have had neither the initiative nor the concern for that kind of thing, but Relling, the prophet of the life-lie, succeeds in convincing him that this is the way in which he really can recoup the family fortune—and without too much effort at that.

From Relling's standpoint, life in accordance with an ideal is far too strenuous an affair; for him, the aim of life is simply to make life bearable, to make the best of a bad lot, and consequently he believes that whatever line of conduct serves that end is justified.

IV

We may see in all this a great many problems. I should like to single out two problems similar to those I mentioned at the outset. One is the concrete and practical problem of whether to tell the whole truth in a specific situation and especially how to communicate this truth so that it will not be misunderstood. In Ibsen's play, this problem is clearly posed in the relations between Gregers and Hialmar. The second problem, one of a more specifically religious nature, is whether it is true that man must live in a lie in order to make life bearable. Let us turn to the former problem first.

When the question of truthtelling is raised most of us are inclined to think at once of the casuistic question: How may the telling of a lie be justified? While it is impossible to avoid making some pronouncement about this way of approach, and especially about the validity of casuistry itself, I do not believe that Ibsen's play actually raises the question in this form. Gregers Werle is not like a man in a resistance movement deciding that a lie to the enemy is justified in a good cause, nor is he in the position of one who is asked by a would-be murderer for information concerning the whereabouts of an intended victim and who decides that only a lie will save his life. Situations of this sort are generally supposed to test the validity of truth and truthtelling and to pose a dilemma for the truthloving person in that they seem clearly to call for a lie, that is, an expression of a conscious intention to deceive, as the only way to achieve some obviously desirable end.

Werle, on the other hand, is in a situation where he is not forced to answer any questions and where there is no external obligation upon him to say anything whatsoever to the Ekdals concerning the truth of his father's past or the former life of Gina Ekdal. Werle, for reasons previously pointed out, simply decides that his former silence, his acquiescence in the face of fraud, was wrong and that he must now expose the truth of the affair if he is to save his friend from further life in a false situation. Telling the truth thus appears to Werle as the only course of action possible if he is to achieve his purpose. His problem is not so much a problem of whether to lie or not, but whether he ought to break his silence and intervene in the lives of his friends at all. From his standpoint, the Ekdals are already in the lie; their lives have long since been determined by the infidelity of old Werle and the willingness of Gina to start anew with Hialmar without telling him the whole truth about her past. Consequently, Gregers sees his chief problem as that of how to repair the damage done by past lies to which he was a party only in the sense that he allowed himself to be silenced. And the course of action upon which he settles is due mainly to his naive reasoning that because falsehood brought so much misery in its wake, revelation of the full truth must somehow set the matter right again.

Even after he had decided to acquaint Hialmar with all the facts surrounding Gina's past, Gregers paid no attention to the subtleties of communication. He either did not care or he did not grasp the significance of Hialmar's consistent failure to make any sense of his talk about the "claim of the ideal." Nor did he take seriously Hialmar's inability to apprehend the symbolic meaning of the duck and his own attempt to play the role of "clever dog." Had young Werle understood all these things, he might have been able to distinguish between communicating the truth to another and simply telling it so that it can be heard. One man may tell another the truth and the hearer may, for one reason or another, be unwilling or unable to receive it for what it is. I have not communicated the truth merely by speaking it; I must, in addition, pay attention to the full situation within which I seek to communicate and, above all, to the nature and capabilities of the one to whom I speak. Gregers was a total failure in all these respects; he did not understand that to put the situation he faced on a truthful basis demanded a course of action more intricate and subtle than the simple one he adopted. Bringing the truth to bear is not the same as just telling it.

It may be objected that our discussion proceeds upon the one assumption most in need of justification, namely, that the truth is always to be told and at all costs. The objection may be admitted; I have purposely blunted the edge of the casuistical question, partly because, as I have indicated, it does not seem to me that the play raises the question in that way, and partly because I seriously doubt the possibility of offering any single rule adequate to the task of guiding human conduct in situations of the sort presented in *The Wild Duck*. There is always a creative element in human decision and action and this element expresses the moral quality of the moral self. Nevertheless, there must be in all moral action a pole representative of stable principle, a standard by reference to which action is to be judged. Even if we refuse to accept casuistical justification of lying, some clear principle is necessary if we are to make any pronouncement about the situation at all.

Deliberate deception, we may say, could be a course of action for us, *if and only if,* we are reasonably sure that the situation satisfies two conditions. First, the end in view, must be such that it clearly outweighs in importance the denial of the validity of truth implicit in such deception. Secondly, the act of deception must be one which may reasonably be expected to achieve, or in some material way contribute to, the desired objective. There are situations in human life where telling the truth and especially what must pass in ordinary situations as the whole truth would result in a state of affairs worse than before. This much must be admitted. Violation, however, of so basic a principle as the universality of truth can be countenanced only with a deep awareness that disloyalty to truth in any instance is an action which ultimately strikes at the heart of the distinction between truth and falsity itself. As soon as we enter into a weighing of the evidence for or against telling the truth in a given case, we are essentially bartering truth and attempting to translate it into a value in exchange. We are attempting to give it a price and when we do that we are implying that truth is a piece of our property which we may keep or withhold at will, depending upon our belief that another person does or does not have the right to the truth we possess. In cases where we think we can see that telling less than the truth will achieve a result which is good, we are inclined to think that talk about the universality of truth and our unqualified commitment to it is rather high flown and that only a hopeless "absolutist" would continue to argue that the lie should not be told. Consider, however, whether there is any logical difference between the case where we deny truth to a man on the ground that he would misuse it if he possessed it, and the case where a government in propaganda denies truth to others on the ground that they would misuse it if they possessed it. In both cases there is a clear identity, namely, the judgment that truth is to be communicated only upon conditions which the one who possesses it can determine. What troubles me in all this, is that the will to truth in our Western tradition, empirical science being one of the most striking expressions of that will, has taught us to regard truth as no man's private property disposable at will upon any conditions a man wants to propose. It may be objected, of course, that the two cases cited are different in character, and I would certainly admit that they are, but, on the other hand, there is the underlying identity in both cases, the principle that truth can be withheld or communicated upon conditions specified by the one who "owns" the truth.

The problems involved are obviously too complex and they involve too lengthy a discussion to be treated here. It is necessary to pass on to the second problem: Is life bearable only if man lives in a lie? Can no man live in the truth?

Whereas the first problem is best illustrated through the relations between Gregers and Hialmar, the second is raised in a striking way by the opposition between Gregers and Relling. This problem is one of greater scope and importance than the first one, for its touches the basis of life itself and is not concerned simply with one detail besides others within life. In this regard it borders upon the religious sphere, for the issue turns on nothing less then the status of man in the cosmos and the type of life possible for him within it. Relling maintains that without some sort of myth—and by "myth" he means a falsehood or explicit deception—no life is bearable. He does not bother with the question of the *good* life, nor is he particularly exercised about what man "ought" to do or to believe; his chief concern is with what is required that man may be able to exist in a measure of comfort and unconcern. It is important to notice that, far from claiming ignorance about the nature and destiny of man in the world, Relling claims to know no less than the truth of the matter. He speaks as one who knows that life is not possible without a life-lie and his main thesis is not that we are in the dark as regards the nature of life, but that the truth is known and it is unbearable. If we are to survive, he concludes, some form of palatable deception about both ourselves and others is indispensable.

Gregers, on the other hand, naive as he may be, is committed to the view that man can and must live in the truth. He is not willing to admit that man's life must ultimately be dependent upon deception. Gregers dares to believe that if man is the one being who is capable of distinguishing clearly between truth and falsehood, and also who has the power to pursue truth through the thicket of prejudice and error, he must, at the very least, attempt to dwell in full awareness and acknowledgment of the truth he can discover. In this respect, Gregers will not sacrifice the dignity of man by retreating into the irresponsibility of cynicism and the superficial comfort of self-deception.

It would, of course, be as great a disaster on the other side of the scale if we were to neglect the dark side of life, to underestimate the weakness of man and his capacity for such deception as will make his life more comfortable. The sad truth is that we do not always find the truth; frequently because we will not. Nor do we always live in sight of the full truth about ourselves and those around us since we have neither the courage nor the faith to do so. Who is there among us, we may ask, who is able to grasp the truth about himself, and who is there possessed of strength enough to live with it without transforming it or without improving upon it where it reveals our shortcomings or distorting it when it reveals the success and perhaps the superiority of others? Who is there who has the courage to welcome the truth and who the steadfastness to resist the temptation to remake the truth into a better likeness of his own personal desires and preferences?

Relling knows full well this aspect of human nature and, under the guise of a realism which hopes to avoid being taken in, he exploits human weakness and folly. His solution is simply to accept our capacity for self-deception and build our life around it. His position, in contrast with that of young Werle, has the merit of acknowledging some tragic facts about the world. But the chief defect in Relling's outlook is that it makes no attempt to pass beyond tragedy; it ignores the fact—as well attested as any other in the world—that man alone among all the animals has the power to distinguish truth from falsity and that consequently he cannot, without the most glaring inconsistency, live as if the distinction made no difference whatever in his life. It is one thing to say that man as he shows himself to be in actual life is weak and scarcely able to face the truth, but it is quite another to make this tragic fact into a principle to which all are inescapably bound. An unrelieved realism must be content to record the fact of human weakness [1] and to describe man and his world as they appear in experience. Realism, however, goes beyond itself (and in the wrong direction) when it demands complete acquiescence in the face of tragic facts. Where man and his nature are concerned, it never follows from the fact that something has been the case in the past that it will be or must be so in the future. There is another and different attitude toward tragic facts, an attitude which deplores that they are so and seeks a way beyond them. If man is capable of knowing truth but not always capable of living in it and with it, the

---

[1] It is a serious question whether a realism which claims to do no more than describe the world as it actually is can legitimately regard any fact about the world as "tragic," since tragedy is a category of interpretation which, like all such categories, takes us beyond fact as such.

solution need not be to live in a lie. A far more fitting solution is to find a source of courage and power which will enable man both to know the truth and to live in it at the same time.

The Wild Duck leaves us with the strange paradox of Relling, the professed realist, who is convinced that man cannot bear the truth and must resort to a life lived on the basis of a great lie, and Gregers Werle, a champion of ideals, who aims above all else at finding out the truth and bringing it to bear upon the situation. The usual view of these two ways of interpreting life is here reversed; the realist is usually portrayed as the one who cuts through lies and sham and exposes life as it "really" is, while the idealist is most frequently painted as a man who cannot face the real world and prefers to live in another world of his own making, the world of his "ideals." Ibsen cleverly brings out the sentimentality most frequently hidden in hard-bitten realism and the uncompromising realism which motivates those who take ideals literally and seriously enough to want to actualize them in the world of time and change.

Both views of life and truth are defective, but it is not difficult to see that the greater error lies in Relling's outlook. The dignity of man, as the Judeo-Christian tradition has always maintained, is to be found in the fact that he is measured and judged by a standard which far exceeds his powers to fulfil while still remaining relevant to his human situation. It is for this reason that it will not do simply to say that man must distort the truth in order to live, for whatever need he may have for deception, the fact remains that man is still the being who can attain to truth and he continues to remain under its judgment. To whom much is given, much will be required; man continues to be the foremost exemplification of this truth. The dignity of man and at the same time the depth of his frailty and willfulness is made manifest by his being held accountable in terms of an ideal which he can never literally realize. It is in this sense that the "claim of the ideal" is a valid claim, despite human weakness and in the face of all forms of realism. So taken, this claim is so powerful that it can make itself felt even through the fumbling and stupidity of Gregers Werle.

VI

THE LINE OF CAPONSACCHI

(Robert Browning: *The Ring and the Book*)

BY

EDWARD DAVISON

When I rashly undertook to talk about the *Line of Caponsacchi,* I had not reread Browning's *Ring and the Book* for nearly twenty years. If I had had my wits about me I would have begged for one of the other assignments in this series, something less strenuous connected with a less bulky work, a moral issue arising out of *The Antigone,* or *Billy Budd* or *The Death in Venice.* At that time and distance the mountain of *The Ring and the Book* looked mole-hillish to me. I awoke later to find myself bewildered and sometimes lost in the mazes of that wonderful but exceedingly intricate and difficult poem, one of the very longest in our language.

The importance and the depth of a great moral issue is, however, not to be gauged by the physical dimensions of the particular literary work from which it emerges. I would not pretend for a moment that the moral problem faced by Caponsacchi is any graver or more difficult than the problems posed by the shorter works of Melville, Sophocles, or Thomas Mann. The problem Browning deals with is of a rather special kind. It is not easy for a Protestant layman like myself to discuss with any very deep understanding the moral dilemma of a Roman Catholic priest who lived in Italy over three centuries ago, one who was subject to sanctions and rules that many of us in this twentieth century in America cannot even begin to appreciate in terms of moral immediacies in another country long ago.

My dilemma in attempting to approach the dilemma of Caponsacchi lies in the difficulty of trying to disengage from the six hundred pages of Browning's masterpiece all the scattered and buried evidence, information, opinion, the shrugs and hints and declarations, with their hundreds of shades and facets and contrarieties, that have to be added and subtracted and multiplied one with another, if I am to make them intelligible to you. A poor hope! I have no means of knowing one very important thing: how many in my audience have any close knowledge of *The Ring and the Book?* Those of you who have read it and know something, more or less, about it will have to bear with me, if I seem to simplify the congestions of the poem. Others must bear with me, if I do not explicate sufficiently. By way of apology I could say that Browning himself had a great deal of trouble in making himself clear to his contemporaries who may have been very much more intelligent and attentive to him than we are, though I cannot vouch for that.

Here, then, is one of the two or three longest poems in the English language, a poem that has been described by a first class critic as probably the most original long poem that was ever written. That would include the *Odyssey* and the *Divine Comedy* and a number of other major poetical works. So I do not see how in a short chapter I can avoid oversimplification. There may be readers who are lifelong scholars of Browning. To them I apologize beforehand for my shortcomings. In fact, I apologize to you one and all. There is no need for me or for you to feel unhappy about all this. I spent several days recently at a meeting of the Modern Language Association and made a spot-check among many of my friends, professors of literature, even scholars in Victorian literature. I found only three men who had anything enlightening to tell me about *The Ring and the Book*. Most of the others admitted that they had not read it since they were undergraduate students; and many confessed that they had never read it at all. It is not an easy work to read. So here we are, you and I together, possibly in a kind of semivacuum of high interest mixed with bewilderment.

I have been reading the poem for several months past, carefully and constantly. It is not my business to discuss the poem or the quality of it, as such. But something must be said about the method of presentation employed by Browning. That, after all, is part of the description of our undertaking in this series.

The narrative (if it may be so called) proceeds by means of a series of multiple monologues dealing with a central situation. That situation is first of all described by the poet in his own character. He talks about his book, about the people who inhabit it; of how he encountered the material of the story. He tells us something about the murders on which the poem is based and something about the trial whereon the monologues are centered. The monologues follow in succession. First the speaker who represents "Half-Rome" and then the "Other-Half Rome," one in sympathy with the husband-murderer, the other in sympathy with the murdered wife. Then comes "Tertium Quid," the voice, cynical and supercilious, of fashionable society, a half-man talking for drawingroom effect, indifferent really to the horror and pity of the situation, blind to its human realities. Tertium Quid is one of those fencesitters, the neutrals who watch the battle but do not take sides much less participate in it, the people whom Dante placed in the lowest circle of his Hell. Tertium Quid is a slavish snob and a prig. And, like many other characters in the works of Robert Browning, he exemplifies and illustrates the point made by one of the poet's most understanding critics who suggested that perhaps the most amazing thing Browning does is that he deals not only with evil in general, but with one of the very greatest of all evils, that is, the behavior of those people to whom good and evil are simply the material in which they trade. They do not care whether the material is good or evil; to them it is "goods," just as cloths and textiles are goods to a dealer who does not care what his clients buy, so long as they buy.

The next monologue is that of the murderer himself, Guido Franceschini, interpreting the story to justify himself and twisting it to suit his hopes of acquittal. He comes fresh from the hands of the torturer and he is talking to save his life. And then we listen to the young priest, Giuseppe Caponsacchi, the character in whom we are chiefly interested, of whom more later. Then to Pompilia, Guido's seventeen year old wife, two weeks a mother, lying on her deathbed, the victim of thirty-five wounds dealt by her husband and his minions with their hooked daggers. And then two monologues by the opposing lawyers in the case, each in his own way trafficking with good and evil in the way of business, each thinking of his professional reputation and neither caring a scrap about Guido or Pompilia so long as he can win his case and his fee and become better known in Rome. Then comes, possibly, the greatest of the twelve books in Browning's poem, the meditation of the aged Pope as he sits alone in his private study in the Vatican. He has been appealed to to determine the case after the court has made its decision, because Guido, the murderer, has pleaded Benefit of Clergy. Then, in the condemned cell, the Pope having rejected his appeal, we return again to Guido in the longest book of the twelve. He has been found guilty and condemned to execution. Three Cardinals sit with him while he awaits the call to execution. He is raving to everybody who might save him, to the Pope, to God, to his fellow countrymen, to the Bishops. But, as he is led out, he cries in the access of his guilt and agony to his murdered wife, "Pompilia will you let them murder me?"

Such is the organization of the poem, the way in which Browning contrived his great work. And out of all this I must try to disengage the moral problem of the priest, Caponsacchi. In order to do just that I must spend a few minutes on the essentials of the story. It is impossible to go into all the multitude of details.

Guido is a nobleman from Arezzo. He is impoverished. He is a very hard, harsh, and self-seeking man in his fifties, swarthy, pitiless, ambitious. Above all, he is greedy for money and he wants to repair his fortunes. Someone suggests to him that here, in Rome, is a very beautiful and eligible young girl, the only daughter of two simple, middle class people who would probably be delighted if he offered to marry her. There is a good deal of money which the girl (Pompilia) will inherit when the old people die. He and his agents approach the mother who consents to the alliance but does not tell her husband of it. The marriage is secretly accomplished—Pompilia does not know what it signifies since she is only thirteen. She complies with her mother's wishes. When her father finds out what has happened he is angry and unhappy: but his wife persuades him to accept the *fait accompli*. There is a lull. A few weeks later Guido comes to claim

Pompilia, who, together with the parents, goes with him to Arezzo to live in Guido's palace where they are very badly and neglectfully treated. Finally they flee the town, leaving Pompilia, miserable, behind them. They return to Rome where the mother goes to law, declaring that Pompilia is not really her child. She thinks her declaration will divert the inheritance for which Guido has married Pompilia, and that, therefore, Guido will release Pompilia. The fact is that Pompilia was the child of a common prostitute who was glad to be rid of her when she was adopted by the putative parents. This information renders Guido furious. He appeals to the court and manages to have the objections set aside. Ultimately he will be able to claim the fortune. From that moment he begins to torment and persecute his young wife who is completely in his power at Arezzo. In the house, living with them, is Guido's brother, a young priest, who makes advances to Pompilia with (apparently) the full knowledge of Guido, the husband. What Guido wants to do is to entrap Pompilia in some way that will disgrace her and enable him to be rid of her and to keep the inheritance. It is at this point that the young priest, Caponsacchi, enters the picture. Guido tries to involve him.

Caponsacchi is a nobleman of Arezzo, the scion of a much older and nobler family than that of Guido. He has entered the priesthood to which he was dedicated from childhood. When we first meet him he is not entirely a dedicated priest. He lived in an age when there was a good deal of license. He flirts with the ladies and does not pay the fullest attention to his sacerdotal responsibilities and duties. But there is nothing very culpable about anything he has done. He is only twenty-four years of age. One day with one of his fellow canons at the theater—the very canon, Guido's brother, who is making advances to Guido's wife—he sees Pompilia for the first time. Guido is there at the back of the box. The canon throws a little paper package of comfits into Pompilia's lap, skipping behind Caponsacchi so that it appears that Caponsacchi had thrown the sweets, which he had not done. Pompilia looks at him and in that moment something happens to him. He idealizes her. She is extremely beautiful, young and shiningly innocent in all her appearance and demeanor. He sees in her the image of womanly purity. As Browning presents it, there is no sexual response on Caponsacchi's part. He is stricken with the appearance of her spiritual character. For some days after the encounter he thinks of her. In the meantime Guido, the husband, who has misinterpreted the incident, plans to entrap his wife with the young priest. Caponsacchi is approached by a woman of Guido's household who carries a letter purporting to come from Pompilia in which Caponsacchi is invited to make an assignation with her. She is (the letter says) in love with him; and her husband is away. Caponsacchi does not credit the letter for a moment. He knows instinctively that Pompilia could not have written such a letter; and he guesses that it was written by Guido. He replies ironically saying that Pompilia must be faithful to a bad husband. The truth of the matter is that Pompilia can neither read nor write. She neither sent nor received the succession of notes that pass between herself and Caponsacchi who will have nothing to do with her. A point comes where, in response to a letter which mentions that Guido has said that if he sees Caponsacchi near his house he will kill him, Caponsacchi (who is not afraid of Guido or of anyone) responds—"Well, I don't want to come to your house; but the street outside doesn't belong to you." He walks down the street and, suddenly, Pompilia from her window balcony speaks to him. She says, in effect, "I have had letters from you. I cannot read or write. I cannot believe, having seen you, that you would be the kind of person who would make these advances, these propositions to me. You are a priest and, presumably, a gentleman. I need your help. I am in danger of my life. I must go back to my mother and father in Rome. I am being persecuted within the walls of my own house. (She is being beaten and ill-treated, too, but she does not say so.) Will you help me to get to Rome?"

We must remember how, in that day and age, it was impossible for a young woman, or indeed any woman, to travel unescorted. She would need a carriage, a coachman, and an escort. She would need to stop by the way. She would have to pass through the gates of a walled city. Pompilia was in a completely helpless situation.

She has already appealed to the only persons who might be able to help her, among them the Archbishop of Arezzo, Caponsacchi's superior in the Church. He has rejected her plea on the grounds that she has married Guido and must take the ill with the good. "You owe him the duty of a wife." She is being ill treated: she is pregnant. She feels that she must escape, not only for her own sake but for the sake of her unborn child.

Caponsacchi listens to her and undertakes to help her. He promises to come the next night. He does not argue with her. He makes no declarations. He simply decides to help her. But when he returns to his home he suffers a change of heart, thinking of what his promise means. If he fulfils it a home will be broken. How can he, a priest, engage himself to run away with a married woman, the wife of a nobleman in his own city? He would be breaking, as the world would see it, his celibate vows, disgracing his family name, and disgracing himself in the eyes of the Church.

Now, Browning, as Leslie Stephen said years ago, and Stephen is one of the critics who understood Browning best, "delighted in exhibiting the high moral instinct which dares to override ordinary convictions, or which is not content with the discharge of obscure duties, or superior to vulgar ambitions and capable of self-sacrifice founded upon pure love and sympathy for human suffering." The plight of Caponsacchi is perhaps the best example of any of Browning's characters who are above expectations, overriding ordinary convictions, and take some great courageous chance in the belief, in the personal faith, that they are doing the right thing.

So, as Caponsacchi sits alone by his fire pondering his problem and deciding that he cannot do this thing because it would be wrong, thinking that if God wishes to work some miracle to save poor Pompilia, then God will order and provide for it. Suddenly it occurs to him that he, perhaps, is called to be the miraculous agent through whom God will work. Nevertheless, he decides to see Pompilia and to tell her that he cannot do what she asks of him. When he sees her she speaks first—and I quote the very lines:

> There she stood—leaned there, for the second time,
> Over the terrace, looked at me, then spoke:
> "Why is it you have suffered me to stay
> Breaking my heart two days more than was need?

Why delay help, your own heart yearns to give?
You are again here, in the selfsame mind,
I see here, steadfast in the face of you,—
You grudge to do no one thing that I ask.
Why then is nothing done? You know my need.
Still, through God's pity on me, there is time
And one day more: shall I be saved or no?"
I answered—"Lady, waste no thought, no word
Even to forgive me! Care for what I care—
Only! Now follow me as I were fate!
Leave this house in the dark tomorrow night,
Just before daybreak:—there's a new moon this eve—
It sets, and then begins the solid black.
Descend," . . .

He tells her what to do and he leaves. From that moment there is no turning back.

He meets her. They take the carriage which he has provided and ride posthaste to Rome. Pompilia will not stop on the way, except once for half an hour when the horses are being changed. Finally, a few miles short of Rome, at a little inn, she is completely overcome with exhaustion and says, in effect, "I must rest now because (she is thinking of her unborn child) I *must* rest now." Caponsacchi agrees and finds her a room at the inn where she is comfortably installed and falls asleep at the limits of exhaustion. He waits in the courtyard and there, Guido, in urgent pursuit finds him. Full of hatred and accusation and every possible kind of ugliness, Guido claims that they have drugged him, stolen his money, and fled in adulterous guilt. At that moment Caponsacchi could have killed him and very nearly yielded to the impulse. Pompilia is awakened and, in her indignation attempts to strike at Guido with his own sword. But the bystanders intervene. Pompilia and Caponsacchi are arrested; but the priest insists on having his case tried by the Church (which is his privilege), and demands to be taken to Rome where, a few days later, the case comes before the same court which afterwards sits on the murder trial. The judges deal very leniently with Caponsacchi. They assume that his behavior is the result of "young blood" and high spirits, that it is a mere peccadillo, a sturdy young fellow sow-ing his wild oats. They wink and smile and put their pens to their lips, but Caponsacchi, in spite of his passionate pleas, cannot make them see the truth—which is that Pompilia is in grave danger of assassination, that Guido is not a wronged husband but a potential murderer. And so, Caponsacchi is relegated to Civita Vecchia, the port of Rome, some thirty miles away from the Holy City—a very mild punishment for his supposed misdeed and he is sentenced to stay there in exile for two or three years. Pompilia is sent to a "hospital" and, soon afterwards, released to the care of her parents. Caponsacchi insists to the court—"This woman is going to be murdered if you don't protect her." But they do not protect her. Her child is born and then, a week or two later, there is a knock at the door in the late night. The father inside asks "Who is it?" A voice answers "Caponsacchi!" The door is thrown gladly open. But it is Guido and three of his hired assassins who enter. They kill the two old people and wound Pompilia beyond any hope of recovery. Then the murderers flee by the road back to Arezzo. They are overtaken sleeping in a stable by the way, arrested, brought to the dungeon and thence to trial.

Such, then, is the main course of events up to the time of the murders and of the trial. Browning, in monologue after monologue, deals directly with the trial, revealing and rerevealing cumulatively, from the various different points of view of the speakers, the motives, actions, and thoughts of the characters, describing, interpreting, analyzing, comparing, discussing in a multitude of ways, evidence and opinions as to their respective guilt and innocence. Pompilia and Caponsacchi emerge in the end as two justified, noble, and magnificent people.

But it is Caponsacchi who concerns us here, *The Line of Caponsacchi*. For the remainder of my dwindling space, after all this exposition, I must try to confine my remarks to him.

At the trial he rises in a kind of righteous wrath to accuse his judges. He makes the most impassioned plea for justice, not for himself, but for Pompilia, the innocent, and Guido, the guilty. Even as he speaks he knows that Pompilia is dying, and he insists that if the court had listened to him and believed him at the previous trial she might have been saved. In a sense the judges are the defendants. So far as our purpose is concerned I hardly need to go further. Guido, of course, is rightly found guilty. He is sentenced to be beheaded and his accomplices to be hanged. The aged Pope decides against the allaying benefit of clergy. He sees Guido's character and motives with the clearest possible vision and sums the situation in a single, climacteric line—"And how should I dare die, this man let live?"

And so to the real point about Caponsacchi's dilemma. I have already discussed it from the point of view of the priest who has a reputation at stake, who is remembering his vows and is attempting to obey, as closely as he knows how, those laws, both human and divine, to which he believes himself committed. I remember for many years recoiling from the popular advertising slogan, "Safety First!" It always seemed to me that there are many more important first things than Safety, which, after all, is only another word for selfishness. But there is a worse phrase, very commonly used in our time— I have felt sick to hear it, as I have many times personally heard it even from the lips of teachers, clergymen, and generals. It is, "Why should I stick *my* neck out?", usually with the accent on the *my*.

Caponsacchi's situation was not in a public way very vulnerable. When Pompilia's appeal first came to him, like a low cry (as it were) from someone hurt and fainting in the twilight at the roadside, there was no special worldly compulsion for him to hear it, much less respond to it. He could so easily have said to himself, as indeed he very nearly did, "Why should I stick my neck out? Why should I get myself involved in this? I am a priest. I have taken certain vows. I know that my superiors in the Church have refused to do what I am being implored to do. If I yield to this entreaty I may easily ruin my reputation, as well as that of Pompilia. Her child will be stamped as mine. I have no personal responsibility." (It should be mentioned, by the way, that in the *Old Yellow Book* from which Browning developed his *Ring and the Book*, Caponsacchi and Pompilia were lovers. That is why, if you have not read Browning's poem it might be better not to read the *Old Yellow Book* first because of the false conceptions it might suggest.

No one, save Pompilia herself, was in a position to blame Caponsacchi if he chose not to hear, much less respond to her appeal. The world was then, as it always seems to have been, populated with unhappy, misunderstood young wives. There were always more such women than there were knights to rescue them. But Caponsacchi heard and answered, over and above Pompilia's cry for help, the voice of his personal conscience and decided, in the end, to run all risks, to defy the conventions, to come to her aid. If he, a priest, should fail to rise to the occasion, who else would rise? He may have thought of the parable of the Good Samaritan (which is most relevant here), though the poem does not mention it. He might so easily have ignored Pompilia. Neither the world nor the Church would have known or cared.

To recognize the nature of a moral dilemma is one thing, to choose sides and act is another. It would be interesting, if there were space, to compare Caponsacchi's dilemma with that of Hamlet. Instead, let me conclude with a different kind of picture which may serve to bring home to us, in our own day and age, the perennial nature of the kind of moral problems that are the subjects of this series of luncheon talks. Some of you may remember—it haunted me for years —a cartoon that appeared, I think, in an early issue of the *New Yorker*. The scene is a city street in broad daylight. An ordinary, respectable citizen (who might be any one of us) is crossing the street near an open manhole out of which has emerged a huge octopus which has seized the man with its tentacles and is slowly dragging him down into the sewer. He is beating at it vainly with his umbrella. A small crowd of passersby is lined along the sidewalk watching the proceedings with an air of fascinated interest; but not one of these people makes the faintest move to help the victim. It is not their business. They do not know who he is and, even if they did know, it would probably make no difference. "Am I my brother's keeper?" "Why should *I* stick *my* neck out?" This citation is a far descent from the sublimities of Browning. But it may serve to point the essential moral. Men and women cannot save their souls by existing as mere nonparticipating spectators in the spiritual battles of life. Too many people are spending too much time watching life, religion, politics, literature, art, as if they were spectators ultimately not concerned with the issues at stake from day to day, year to year, generation to generation. They may be intensely interested, thrill to the spectacle in the arena; but their mood and attitude is no more than that of the audience watching a motion picture or a television show or listening to a radio program. Life, other people's lives, are not their business. They are nonparticipants. Only a few weeks ago, a well known man, a friend of mine, was suddenly bludgeoned and robbed in broad daylight with hundreds of people around and not a hand was stretched out to save him or to capture the robber. This kind of thing is a daily occurrence. There was a time when a policeman in pursuit of his duty could count on some people coming to his aid if he called for it. I can understand an underpaid bank teller or a cashier in a store not choosing to risk his life to prevent his employer's money from being stolen by thugs. Nevertheless, we all, I think, do admire the man who puts up a fight. And there is something still, I think, in *noblesse oblige*. I am never sure of what I would do in some of these situations: but I do know what I hope I would do. And I hope it would be the kind of thing that Caponsacchi did. "Is it nothing to you, all ye that pass by?"

VII

THE CEREMONY OF INNOCENCE

(Herman Melville: *Billy Budd*)

BY

WILLIAM YORK TINDALL

Billy Budd seems to make something almost too tidy out of what remains uncertain in *Moby Dick*. Melville's story of the captain, the villain, and the tar, apparently less a story than a commentary on one, may strike the hasty reader as a product of reason rather than imagination, as something reduced to discourse for ready apprehension by basic Englishmen. What had to be said has been said by Captain Vere or Melville himself. As critics, therefore, we may feel frustrated, as Romantics we may prefer a little teasing mystery around, and as esthetes, confronted with discourse, we are sure that talking about a thing is less admirable than embodying it in image or action. Of Kierkegaard's three categories, the esthetic, the moral, and the divine, Melville seems to have chosen the second—to the applause of some and the departure of others, for *Don Giovanni* maybe.

That the matter of *Billy Budd* gratifies what Melville calls "the moral palate" is plain from the plainest rehearsal. The scene is a British frigate during the Napoleonic wars. Two mutinies have justified fears of more. Against this ominous background, Billy, an innocent aboard, is accused for no good reason by Claggart, a petty officer, of plotting mutiny. The captain, a reasonable man, doubts Claggart's story and brings Billy in to confront his lying accuser. Overcome by a stutterer's indignation, the innocent foretopman, unable to speak a word, strikes Claggart dead with a fist like a ham. Captain Vere is faced with a dilemma. Though he believes in Billy's innocence, naval law and prudence alike demand punishment for the

73

impetuous seaman while pity and reason counsel mercy. Internal debate inclines the captain toward conviction, and Billy, condemned despite the "troubled conscience" of his judges, is hanged.

The subject is a quandary or what Melville calls "the intricacies involved in the question of moral responsibility." As the captain ponders "the moral phenomenon presented in Billy Budd" and the "elemental evil" of Claggart, he fathoms the "mystery of iniquity." The case of Billy seems, as the captain says, a matter for "psychologic theologians."

Although, as T. S. Eliot observes in *After Strange Gods,* "It is . . . during moments of moral and spiritual struggle . . . that men [in fiction] . . . come nearest being real," Billy and Claggart, who represent almost pure good and pure evil, are too simple and too extreme to satisfy the demands of realism; for character demands admixture. Their all but allegorical blackness and whiteness, however, are functional in the service of Vere's problem, and Vere, goodness knows, is real enough. Claggart is black because, as Philipp G. Frank once observed, a sinner is necessary for the realization of a moral code; and an innocent is almost equally instructive. These abstractions, a sacrifice of verisimilitude to tactical necessity, reveal the "moral quality" of the captain's mind, which becomes a theater for contending opposites and eventual choice. Such dramatic crises are not only the favorite stuff of novelists but of philosophers and poets as well: Kierkegaard wrote *Either/Or* and Yeats "The Choice."

Not only rational, Vere's choice involves his whole sensitive, adult being. Agony shows on his face as he emerges from his interview with Billy, and a final exclamation shows how deeply he is stirred. Involving more than black and white, the captain's choice is between two moral codes, military and natural. The first is evident; the second is either that of the noble savage, in whom Melville was interested, or what Western culture takes for granted. In other words, the captain's conflict is between the balanced claims of justice and equity, order and confusion, law and grace, reason and feeling, or, as Melville puts it, "military duty" and "moral scruple." Vere's eloquent and moving speech to the drumhead court, the climax of such drama as there is, leaves little to add about these issues and his dilemma.

The conflict of military with natural may occupy the stage, but Melville recognizes other codes, that of custom or respectability, for example. Claggart's "natural depravity" appears in respectable guise. Melville also recognizes the cultural, psychological, and absolute bases for morality, and hints in a very modern way at their operation.

"Moral," Melville's favorite word—in this book at least—is one which, though commonly taken for granted, is slippery. I have read a thing in which "moral" means something else on every page. What Yvor Winters means by it escapes me. Vague and general like F. R. Leavis's "awareness of life" or narrow and definite like the *quid agas* of Scholastic philosophers, the word needs fixing before use. As I shall use it and as I think Melville did, morality implies not only action but motive, attitude, and being. It involves a sense of obligation to self, community, and the absolute, which provide a frame by conscience, law, tradition, or revelation. If we demand a single equivalent, Melville's "responsibility" will do.

Vere's action, however sudden and whether we approve of it or not, is plainly responsible. Billy and Claggart act, to be sure: one bears false witness and the other delivers a blow, but neither actor follows reason and each is more important for what he is than what he does. If being as well as action can be moral, however, they are moral figures, too, existing like cherubs or fiends in a moral atmosphere. Good and bad, they occupy the region of good and evil.

It is agreed by most that moral substance is necessary for the novel. Not the pure form of Flaubert's desire, and falling far short of the condition of music, the novel is an arrangement of references to vital issues, without which it is empty. A value of Joyce's *Ulysses,* for example, is the feeling and idea of charity. That moral substance fails to insure greatness, however, is proved by the works of Horatio Alger; and that it fails to guarantee moral effect is proved by those of Mickey Spillane. The errors of censors and formalists show the folly of judging by morality alone or arrangement alone. Not moral idea but its embodiment in what Eliot called objective correlatives, suitably arranged, determines value. Far from inciting action as moralizing does, embodied morality invites contemplation, and to become an object of contemplation, substance must be distanced by form. The question is not how much morality is there but how much is under control, how fully insight and moral intelligence have submitted to esthetic discipline. Our problem, then, is not morality itself but moral art or morally significant form.

Captain Vere's speech to the court adequately embodies the idea of "moral responsibility" in dramatic form; but we must find if Billy's history has found fitting embodiment. At first reading, that history seems a curious and eccentric structure of essays on ethics, digressions or "bypaths," character sketches, and chronicles of the navy, an arrangement that after uncertain progress tails inconclusively off. Such image and action as we find, failing to halt the lamentable decline, seem occasions for analysis or digression, like biblical texts in a pulpit. Since the crucial interview between Vere and Billy is disappointingly offstage, Melville seems to have avoided the dramatic possibilities of his theme. That the book calls for the dramatization he failed to give it, is proved by attempts at play and opera, which, while affirming excellence of theme, imply that action or image are better ways of presenting it. But something that continues to fascinate us in its present form and calls forth responses beyond the capacity of discourse, suggests art of another kind. Maybe Melville avoided drama in the interests of a less obvious medium.

Moby Dick assures us that Melville was an artist, not a lecturer on ethics. He not only worked three years on *Billy Budd,* but he seems to have regarded the result with far from senile favor. The first version, recently detected in manuscript by F. Barron Freeman, reveals more action and less discourse; yet this version, which corresponds more happily to what we think fiction should be, is not so effective as the one before us with all its weight of digression and analysis.

That Melville was aware of form is clear from passages in *Billy Budd.* When Captain Vere says, "With mankind forms, measured forms, are everything," he probably means usage and custom; but Melville himself, applying Vere's remark to esthetics, says that the symmetry of form desirable in pure fiction cannot be achieved in factual narrative like this. The story is not factual in fact. But Melville, wanting it to seem so, excuses apparent formlessness as a form for giving the illusion of a bare report; for truth, he continues, will always have its ragged edges and matters of fact must lack the finish of an "architectural finial." Aware of loose structure and inconclusive ending, he justifies them for what seem wrong reasons. Not reasons, however, but what he made must detain us while we scout further possibilities. The curious form he made may be functional and, for all our hasty impression and his explanation, effective. Is the book as shapeless as he implies? Or, if shapeless, is shapelessness a kind of shape? Is the book as pedestrian, discursive, and factual as he claims and as we had supposed on first looking into it?

What seems at first to be factual is presented, we find, in part by images and allusions that are incompatible with a pretense of factuality. Though unapparent, those images are livelier than we thought. Consider the coloring of the scene between decks before the execution as Billy lies in white amid profound blackness. Catching up the abstract whiteness and blackness of Billy and Claggart, this image of black and white embodies them. At the execution the rosy dawn that seems "the fleece of the Lamb of God seen in mystical vision" promises a kind of renewal while implying much else. Circling birds after the burial at sea offer by the aid of tradition some spiritual import. And that spilt soup, perhaps more action than image, carries suggestions beyond the demands of plot, suggestions so indefinite, what is more, that they confound its rational progress. Even the names of ships, though serving a more comprehensible purpose, are as significant as those in *Moby Dick*. Billy is removed from the *Rights of Man,* for instance, and Vere is mortally wounded by a shot from the *Athéiste.*

The words of *Billy Budd* carry more than denotation. "Sinister dexterity," at once witty and desolating, sounds like something from *Finnegans Wake,* where, indeed, it reappears. Vere's last words, "Billy Budd," are equivocal. Do they imply feeling, regret, self-realization, understanding? Are they a form for something incompletely realized? However "factual" the words of this pseudoreport, they function like the words of poetry.

Not only last words and indeterminate images but a number of hints about Billy's "all but feminine" nature plague our assumptions.

Roses and lilies dye his cheeks. He comports himself like a "rustic beauty" at times and like a vestal virgin at others. These qualities and appearances, astonishing in an able seaman, calling forth an "ambiguous smile" from one or another of his shipmates, suggest psychological depths and motives below the level of the plain report. By virtue of such intimations Billy seems at once more and less bottomless than we had supposed, and so do the motives of Claggart, if not those of the captain himself. Among such suggestions, avoidance of the obviously dramatic becomes implicit embodiment that escapes the limits of drama.

What pleases me most, however, is the accompaniment of biblical allusions which, however unobtrusive and irregular, recurs like Wagnerian *leitmotiv.* Time and again Billy is compared to Adam and Jesus. Billy's innocence is as much that of Adam before the Fall as that of the more secular noble savage. As a "peacemaker," a term implying beatitude, Billy seems destined for "crucifixion"; and his hanging, condensing events, becomes an ascension. Vere is compared to Abraham about to sacrifice Isaac, obeying God's will with fear and trembling. Becoming a shadow of God, Vere weighs the claims of Adam and Satan. Claggart, whose denunciation is reported in Mosaic terms as "false witness," is compared not only to the Serpent of Eden but to Ananias and to one struck dead by an angel of God, "yet," as the captain says, "the angel must hang!" Man's fall and redemption and all troubles between seem suggested by this large though not fully elaborated analogy, which, bringing to mind the mythical parallels in *Ulysses* and *The Waste Land,* removes Billy a little farther from the abstraction to which, for all his stutter and those rosy cheeks, he seems committed. However incapable of supporting this mythical burden, he becomes by its aid almost as portentous as choosing Vere. The sailors, whose testimony cannot be ignored, are more impressed by Billy than by Vere, reason and all. Not only being and secular victim, Billy becomes saint and martyr and his hanging an omen. Pieces of the spar to which he quietly ascends are venerated like pieces of the true cross, suitable for reliquaries or the holiest of duffle bags. By the aid of myth and military ritual the story of Billy, transformed from an essay on good, evil, and choice, approaches what Yeats called "the ceremony of innocence."

We must conclude that Melville avoided the attractions of the obvious in the interests of indefinite suggestiveness and myth. His work, whatever its air of the factual and the discursive, is symbolist and richer for scarcity of drama and image. Such drama and images as are there function more intensely in their abstract context than profusion could. That the structure as a whole also serves esthetic purpose is likely. As we have seen, the book is a queer arrangement of discourse, action, image, and allusion, with discourse predominating. We have seen how image and action work in this mixture; but we must examine the function of discourse. In such context, discourse, increasing tension, makes allusion and image dramatic or enlarges them, and, working with allusion, image, and action may produce a third something by juxtaposition as in Eliot's *Four Quartets* or Wallace Stevens' *Notes Toward a Supreme Fiction*. Seeming now a structure of conflicts, not only of men and codes but of methods, which become a technical echo of the theme, the book emerges as a structural drama or a drama of structure. An ending that seemed weak afterthought (and was not there in the first version) now unifies all. Vere's exclamation, the saint's legend, and inconclusiveness, working together, comprise a form, which may tail off but tails suggestively off, leaving endless reverberations in our minds. There is more mystery around than we had thought, and we may agree with dying Gertrude Stein that answers are less important than questions. What at a superficial reading had the appearance of exhaustive discourse becomes inexhaustible. The shapeless thing becomes suggestive shape. Neither as loose nor as tight as it once seemed, the strange sequence of precise discourse and indefinite suggestiveness corresponds to our experience of life itself. That the form Melville made fascinates while it eludes and teases is shown no less by popular favor than by the abundance of critical comment.

However different it looks, *Billy Budd* is not altogether different in kind from *Moby Dick,* another structure of digression, discourse, action, and image. The proportions and impact may be different, the images of *Moby Dick* may be more compelling, but both serve symbolic suggestion and both are forms for offering a vision of reality. Not the tidy discourse of our first impression, the work is almost as inexplicable as *Moby Dick*.

What exactly does this form present? It is impossible to answer this question for any symbolist work; for works of this kind escape discursive accounting. We may say that *Billy Budd* is a vision of man in society, a vision of man's moral quandary or his responsibility; but its meaning is more general than these, and that is why it haunts us. So haunted, I find the work not an essay on a moral issue but a form for embodying the feeling and idea of thinking about a moral issue, the experience of facing, of choosing, of being uneasy about one's choice, of trying to know. Not a conclusion like a sermon, *Billy Budd* is a vision of confronting what confronts us, of man thinking things out with all the attendant confusions and uncertainties. Disorder is a form for this and the apparently formless book a formal triumph. To do what it does it has to be a fusion of tight-loose, shapeless-shaped, irrelevant-precise, suggestive-discursive—a mixture of myth, fact, and allusion that has values beyond reference. The discursive parts represent our attempts at thinking, while the action, images, and allusions represent what we cannot think but must approximate. Arrangement of these discordant elements forms a picture of a process.

From my guess at meaning it follows that the center of this form is neither Vere nor Billy but rather the teller of the story or Melville himself. Though ghostlier, he is not unlike the Marlow of Conrad's *Lord Jim* and *Heart of Darkness* or the Quentin of Faulkner's *Absalom, Absalom!* Using Vere and Billy as materials, Melville's thought-process, like those of Marlow and Quentin, is the heart of this darkness and its shape the objective correlative, a form for something at once imperfectly understood and demanding understanding. Morality, the substance of this form, becomes an element that limits and directs the feelings and ideas created by the whole. Moral substance, what is more, may be what engages our minds while the form does its work. Value, not from morality alone, issues from the form that includes it and in which it serves. If the form concerned less, I repeat, it would be trivial, but without its formal presentation the morality would remain in Sunday school.

United now, the beautiful and the good create a vision larger than either, a vision transcending the case of Billy Budd or the quandary of Captain Vere. The teller, now any man, presents man's feeling in the face of any great dilemma. Thought and feeling, outdistancing themselves, become objects of contemplation, remote yet immediate. The effect of this form is moral in the sense of enlarging our awareness of human conditions or relationships and of improving our sensitivity. In such a form Kierkegaard's esthetic, moral, and divine become a single thing.

VIII

CAN ONE SELL ONE'S SOUL?

(The Faust Legend)

BY

HENRY HATFIELD

There are literally hundreds of legends and literary works which are directly or indirectly bound up with the Faust theme. Some, like the stories of Simon Magus and Theophilus of Adana, long antedate the historical Dr. Faust, a German charlatan and adventurer who flourished—if that is the proper word—in the first decades of the sixteenth century. Other versions seem as contemporary as today's newspaper: a very recent French film appropriately connects the Faust theme with the atomic bomb. I intend, after giving a brief account of the famous German *Faustbook* of the late sixteenth century, to concentrate on the treatments of the theme by Marlowe, Goethe, and Thomas Mann. All three try to answer, though in radically different ways, the question which is my theme in this paper; in all three "selling one's soul" is associated with a pact or wager with the devil. We shall observe how the tragic answer of Marlowe gives way, some two hundred years later, to the profound optimism of Goethe; and how Thomas Mann, writing in a time of troubles, repudiates Goethe, returns to tragedy, but finally avoids after all the traditional verdict of utter damnation.

First, though, it will be appropriate to consider the "classic" statement of the legend: the German chapbook of 1587. Freely translated into English some five years later, it became Marlowe's source; it stands at the beginning of the German tradition leading to Goethe; and Mann drew from it heavily in his turn.

The very question, "Can One Sell One's Soul?", suggests at once the world of medieval Christianity: a tripartite world, with God and His angels above, the devil with his insidious cohorts below, and man between the two great hosts. His brief life on this earth is precarious but tremendously dramatic: on his actions and attitudes, during a short career, depends his salvation or damnation for all eternity. For his soul is immortal and uniquely valuable. Small wonder that the infernal powers should plot to gain possession of man's "eternal jewel"; small wonder, given their hellish ingenuity and man's heritage of original sin, that they should often be successful.

Yet the question persists: in this traditional Christian world, why should a man of high intelligence bargain away, as Dr. Faust does, the promise of unending bliss for a mere twenty-four years of earthly experience? Why should he sign a pact which seems absurdly unequal, and do so despite repeated warnings? The motives of the sixteenth century Faust or Faustus are complicated, but they may lead us to the heart of the matter. First, there is the lure of excessive power, gained through illicit means, through magic. As a magician, Faust is already a dubious person, more vulnerable to temptation than other men. Through his art, he obtains superhuman status, limited of course to a definite time. Having entered upon the fateful contract, he can range over Europe and Asia, fly into interstellar space, conjure up the shades, visit Hell, and summon the most beautiful woman who ever lived to be his concubine. These are no mean temptations; yet he has other reasons beyond them for his choice, motives deriving ultimately from the Renaissance spirit which had been sweeping up into northern Europe for about a century. There is the skepticism of the independent mind: despite moments of Christian repentance and fear, Faust often thinks that the devil is not as black as the Church paints him. There is Luciferian pride: in this case, the pride of the intellectual, all the more dangerous because it is founded on real gifts of mind and imagination. Finally, and most significantly, Faust is obsessed by intellectual curiosity. He must learn everything; he must, at any cost, eat again of the Tree of Knowledge. This desire appears blurred by other, less noble drives in the original legend, where no sharp line between magic and rational knowledge is drawn. Yet even here Faust stipulates that "the spirit should tell him nothing but that which is true." [1] In his search for truth lies the inherent nobility of Faust. Coupled with his Titanic ambition, it raises him above other men and ultimately dashes him to perdition. His lust of knowing—*libido sciendi* [2]—drives him to violate the boundaries laid down by God. Yet for all his arrogance, a certain greatness of soul makes him undeniably attractive to his fellow men. Even the author of the original chapbook, an orthodox Lutheran, severely anti-Faustian, tells us of the touching admiration and concern felt by Faust's students for their intellectual guide. Repentance in time could still save him, but even in moments of fear he is incapable of true contrition, feeling like Cain that his offense is too great to be forgiven him. Damnation is inevitable, and the *Faustbook* ends with a stern moral warning. Yet, perhaps unconsciously, the author of the chapbook had sowed the seeds of sympathy for the magician. In Marlowe's drama, this sympathy is already explicit and pervasive.

Marlowe

Marlowe was immediately attracted by the theme: he seems to have begun planning his drama as soon as the legend was available in English. In contrast to the author of the *Faustbook*, the Elizabethan dramatist was strongly in sympathy with the Titanic drives and ambitions of the German magician. Not only was Marlowe a man of the Renaissance; he tended to choose as his dramatic heroes supermen whose tragic fall is due to an overabundance of strength or ambition. Nor could Faust's religious doubts have alienated Marlowe, who was notorious in his time as an atheist, though a recent authority holds that actually he adhered to what we vaguely call "natural religion" or "free-thinking" today. [3] University trained and classically educated, Marlowe naturally inclined to identify himself with Faustus, the intellectual and learned "speculator about the elements." Finally,

---

[1] Spies, *Faustbook*, quoted in Palmer and More, *Sources of the Faust Tradition*, Oxford University Press, New York, 1936, p. 139.

[2] See Harry Levin, *The Overreacher*, Harvard University Press, Cambridge, 1952, p. 27.

[3] *Ibid.*, p. 2.

and most significantly, he endowed his Dr. Faustus with his own burning love of beauty; and precisely here lies his greatest contribution to the legend. In a word, the heroism, rather than the sinfulness of Faustus, is now stressed.[4] Why then should Marlowe, after ennobling his Faustus and attributing to him so much that is admirable, and many qualities germane to his own nature, consign him to perdition after all? Could a poet who presumably agreed with the impatient outburst of his Faustus, "I think Hell's a fable!" have thought that "selling one's soul" to an unreal devil was really a fatal offense? Before venturing an answer, let us consider the drama itself, *The Tragical History of Dr. Faustus*.

Broadly speaking, Marlowe followed the plot of the English *Faustbook* very closely. He retained even the coarse tricks and practical jokes which play such a large part in the legend, assigning them in typical Elizabethan fashion to a comic underplot. Essentially, he makes two great changes: by deepening the motivation of his Faustus he makes him more credible; by ennobling his character, he renders him more tragic. His Faustus has mastered the four faculties of conventional knowledge and found them wanting: he sums up the situation in lines which remarkably anticipate Goethe:

> Philosophy is odious and obscure;
> Both law and physic are for petty wits;
> Divinity is basest of the three,
> Unpleasant, harsh, contemptible, and vile:
> 'Tis magic, magic that hath ravished me.
> (Act I, ll. 107–111)

Faustus's desire for infinite knowledge is essentially an expression of the will to superhuman power typical of Marlowe's heroes; "A sound magician is a demigod," he exclaims. No "pure" intellectual, he is moved in part by the promise "of honour and of wealth" (Act II, l. 22). A child of the Renaissance, Faustus still partially believes in Christian theology. Marlowe well symbolizes his dilemma by placing him between a Good Angel and a Bad, the latter of course playing the role of tempter. The Good Angel has no chance; Faust brushes away

---

[4] Havelock Ellis, introduction to *Christopher Marlowe*, Mermaid Series, Benn, London, 1948, p. xxxviii.

"fears of hell or hopes of paradise." Willing the end, he must will the means. (One recalls that Marlowe's contemporaries charged him with Machiavellianism.) [5] Until too late, he ignores all the warnings and suppresses the voices of conscience and anxiety. Yet he remains generally admirable: he scours the universe for knowledge and for adventure, less attracted by hedonistic debauchery than his legendary predecessor had been. Even when he makes the Pope and his cardinals the butt of low comedy, we sense rather a concession to Protestant prejudice than a real loss of stature. In the encounter of Faustus with Helen of Troy, Marlowe has transmuted what had been a mere episode into the poetic zenith of the drama, a Renaissance invocation of beauty. This beauty Faustus would never have known, unless he had "sold his soul."

Faustus, though, is tragically in error; he realizes soon enough that he is in a Christian universe. God is not mocked. Mephistophilis tells him that hell is not only real; it exists wherever a damned soul may be found. Repeatedly, Faustus tries to repent; toward the end, he loses his nerve completely. His last words: "I'll burn my books!— Ah, Mephistophilis!" have a particularly sinister ring to the twentieth century ear. The chorus points the moral:

> Cut is the branch that might have grown full straight,
> And burned is Apollo's laurel-bough,
> That sometime grew within this learned man.
>
> (Epilogue, ll. 1–3)

The Elizabethan audience had but one answer to our question: a magician can of course sell his soul—who else, indeed, would be as likely to do so?—and his punishment would then be thoroughly deserved. What of Marlowe's "private" answer to the question? In a sense, we have no right to ask: he was writing drama, not theology or philosophy, and he could not do without a tragic fall. Yet certainly we are not forcing the text when we sense in it a sympathy for Faustus's doubts, as well as for his intellect, his imagination, and his ambitions. Perhaps there is also a note of humanistic protest against the dreadful —and orthodox—severity implied: "punishment in eternity for a sin

[5] Levin, *op. cit.*, pp. 2 f.

committed in time." [6] The undeniable intensity of Faust's final despairing speech may be revealing. Perhaps, like so many men after him, Marlowe was an unbeliever only in his conscious mind; perhaps ". . . there lingers [here] at least an echo of the boyish faith of a meditative lad, wondering and growing up in the dim, religious atmosphere of ancient Canterbury. . . ." [7] It may, however, be significant that when Faustus, in an agony of fear, implores the horses of night to run slowly—

> *O lente, lente currite, noctis equi!*

he is quoting Ovid's appeal that a night of love be prolonged. At any rate, the humanist Marlowe must have sensed the irony of citing such a source at such a moment. While there is no ambiguity whatsoever about *Dr. Faustus* as a tragedy, as a work of art taken solely on its own terms, it leaves us unclear about Marlowe's own spiritual commitments.

Goethe

In Goethe's *Faust,* this state of things is directly reversed. The German drama is full of ironies; we are not even sure why Goethe called it a tragedy; but there can be no real doubt about the intellectual statement which Goethe intended here: an assertion of faith in man, and more particularly in the fundamental goodness of the active element in man's nature. [8]

In *Faust,* the product of a process of poetic endeavor extending intermittently over some sixty years, Goethe appears as the heir of several great movements in European thought. He is indebted to the Enlightenment for his belief in the basic goodness of the universe. Goethe is particularly close to the philosopher Leibnitz in his belief

---

[6] See E. M. Butler, *The Fortunes of Faust,* The University Press, Cambridge, England, 1952, p. 48.

[7] John Bakeless, *The Tragicall History of Christopher Marlowe,* Harvard University Press, Cambridge, 1942, vol. I, p. 140.

[8] I am aware of recent "negative" readings of the poem, but remain unconvinced. See B. Q. Morgan's marshaling of the evidence in *Symposium,* vol. VIII, 1954, pp. 102–112.

in the magnificent harmony of the universe, which he expressed in the tremendous lines of the Prologue in Heaven. Leibnitz's notion that the soul of man is a monad, a spiritual atom, endowed with an innate upward drive, clearly anticipates the "eternally striving" soul of Goethe's Faust. Another German of the Enlightenment, Lessing, planned a *Faust* in which the hero was to be saved: "God has not endowed man with the noblest of all instincts [the desire for truth] in order to render him eternally wretched," [9] the angel proclaims in Lessing's fragment. But rationalistic faith in reason did not of itself satisfy Goethe, who found the pure intellectual a comic and frustrated figure. He took from Rousseau the belief in the virtue of unspoiled natural emotions—"feeling is everything," Faust says—and combined the two strains, affirming human nature in its totality. Neither reason nor feeling is adequate in itself. From Herder he learned that all life, from the plants to man, is involved in an unending upward development; from Winckelmann, that Greek art represented the pinnacle of human achievement. Thus his Helen, like Marlowe's, became a symbol of absolute beauty. It will be observed that all of these doctrines have a strongly affirmative cast; and that Leibnitz, Lessing, and Herder conceive of history as a dynamic upward movement.

But what of evil? what of tragedy? For all his long range optimism, Goethe was far from ignoring evil and suffering in human life. His Faust commits a series of ruthless acts; his Gretchen perishes miserably. The element of negativity and destruction enters of course in Mephistopheles, "the spirit who always denies." Mephisto is a very complicated devil, part eighteenth century rationalist, wit, and man of the world; part an embodiment of darkness warring against light, of the destructive powers of nature struggling against creativity. He is a highly intelligent, cynical, and at times formidable opponent; but he is hopelessly mistaken about the nature of the universe. As the drama goes on, he increasingly loses stature, sinking at times to the role of the fool; he is hopelessly defeated. Evil appears as a necessary element of the cosmos, but a relatively minor one. In different terms, we can say that Goethe simply did not believe in a principle of radical evil, either in human nature or in the universe. At one time, Goethe

[9] *Lessings Faustdichtung,* edited by R. Petsch, Winter, Heidelberg, 1911, p. 47.

even half-seriously considered reversing the tradition completely, and letting Mephisto himself be pardoned! [10]

It will probably be objected that Faust after all does sell his soul. Looking at the drama, we find first an implied wager between God and Mephistopheles: as in Job, God gives the devil a free hand with an exemplary man, but only as long as he is on the earth. At the same time, He expresses complete certainty of Faust's ultimate salvation, stating also that Faust will err as long as he strives. Error is not of course good in itself, but it is paradoxically the condition and indication of activity, and hence ultimately of good. A nonerring man would be spiritually dead. All this is too dialectical for Mephistopheles, who ignores it, blithely confident that he can outwit Omniscience. As the drama proper begins, we find a Faust reminiscent of Marlowe's; though of a more complicated psychological makeup. A great scholar, a disillusioned intellectual, he has become convinced of the futility of any attempt to grasp the truth through rational means. Faust is searching for nothing less than a state of absolute insight, an experience which will satisfy both his intellectual and his nonrational strivings. "Knowledge" would be too narrow a word for his goal, which he symbolizes in the expression "the fair moment"—*der schoene Augenblick*. Frustrated in an attempt to gain understanding of nature through a feat of white magic, he comes close to suicide. Perhaps death will open the door to the absolute, he suggests in a despairing monologue; but the will to live is too strong. Faust is thus thrice frustrated, and Mephisto, believing the time is ripe, approaches him. The bargain which ensues is actually a conditional pact or wager. If Faust ever relapses into hedonistic ease, if indeed he ever accepts any experience as complete and satisfying, he has lost. The pact is signed, and the two set out on their adventures.

The events of the first part of the drama, culminating in the tragedy of Gretchen, are too familiar to recount here. In the second part, largely the product of Goethe's later years, the poem changes its character radically. *Faust II* is broader in scope, more intellectual and less emotional in tone than the First Part. Generally the Second Part,

[10] H. G. Graef, *Goethe ueber seine Dichtungen*, 2 Teil, vol. II, Ruetten & Loening, Frankfurt a.M., 1904, pp. 226 f.

concerned as it is with the development of Western man, and of life itself, moves deliberately; but it has passages of great intensity. The action moves from Germany to Greece, from the sixteenth century to the Homeric age, and back. Faust has become more mature, more cultivated, clearer about his own motives; but his basic character has changed little if at all. He is as dynamic as ever, and as ruthless. His union with Helena is a symbolic synthesis of the modern and the classical worlds, of Germany and Greece. If the terms of the bargain had been strictly enforced during this idyll, Faust would surely have lost, for the Greek "moment" is fair indeed; but Goethe, interested here in broad cultural questions, found it convenient to ignore the pact for the time being. Perhaps such a specifically Christian arrangement loses its validity in mythological Greece.

Returned to northern Europe, the agéd Faust undertakes his final exploit, the reclamation of land from the sea. Colonization replaces cultural exploration. Still intensely active, still erring, he commits his gravest offense but rises, immediately after his crime, to his most heroic stature. An old couple, touchingly innocent adherents of outmoded beliefs, possesses land which Faust covets. He commissions Mephistopheles to remove them to another location; force is employed, and they are killed. Immediately after the deed, Faust is attacked by Care, the spirit of torturing self-doubt and anxiety. He could perhaps banish Care by employing magical means, but refuses to do so; it is an indication that his long delayed moral maturity is at last at hand. She blinds him, but he magnificently defends his spiritual freedom: the light within burns more brightly than ever. With renewed energies, about to throw himself again into his enterprise, he has a vision of a great social future:

> And such a throng I fain would see,
> Stand on free soil among a people free!
> Then dared I hail the Moment fleeing:
> *"Ah, still delay—thou art so fair!"*
> In proud fore-feeling of such lofty bliss,
> I now enjoy the highest Moment. . . .[11]

[11] Bayard Taylor's translation of *Faust II*, Osgood, Boston, 1875, p. 295.

But these are Faust's last words on earth; he dies, and Mephisto, sure that he has won the wager, summons his minions to carry Faust's soul away to hell.

Mephistopheles is wrong again, of course; angels descend suddenly, drive off the devils with a celestial bombardment, and carry Faust's soul to heaven. In the last, amazing scene, the action moves vertically upward; Faust, purified and forgiven, rises higher and higher, drawn by the "eternal feminine," woman being Goethe's characteristic symbol of love and healing. Thus the drama, permeated though it is with pantheistic, evolutionary, and pagan elements, ends in a Christian mystery—or better, a mystery which employs Christian imagery. One tends to agree with Santayana: Faust is too restless to stay long in Heaven, and will soon set off on new adventures.[12]

There has been endless and largely futile debate on the justness or unjustness of Faust's salvation. Technically, he is saved by a hair's breadth; he utters the fateful words only in anticipation. Goethe remarked that Mephisto half-wins, half-loses the wager; then God makes use of His right of pardon to resolve the issue.[13] In any event, few readers will feel that the exact terms of the bargain are very important; Faust's dynamic drive continues to the very end, and that is decisive. As Barker Fairley puts it: ". . . the poem . . . says and says again that the active impulse is good and that we must trust it." [14] We may indeed go further: in this context, the notion of "selling one's soul" has no ultimate meaning. In Goethe's view, the soul or entelechy of a significant man—that is, the organization of his intellectual and spiritual powers—is indestructible and inalienable. The soul is the man himself. Faust, in other words, was merely wagering that he would remain Faustian; by definition, he could not lose. In my view, the pact is a useful device to get the great poem under way; it is no longer really central, as it is in the legend.

Many will protest that the really staggering optimism of the poem is unacceptable. Goethe seems here to underrate the perversity of

[12] George Santayana, *Three Philosophical Poets,* Harvard University Press, Cambridge, 1945, p. 188.

[13] Graef, *op. cit.,* p. 272. The tone of Goethe's words here is remarkably ironic: "das Begnadigungs-Recht des alten Herrn."

[14] Barker Fairley, *Goethe's Faust,* Clarendon Press, Oxford, 1953, p. 121.

human nature, to deny the existence of damnation, to reduce evil to error, and error in turn to a mere function of action. To this one must reply that the poem does not gloss over human suffering or wrong-doing, nor does it hide from us the cost of a career like Faust's. Faust is not Goethe's ideal; he represents one aspect of it: individualism, activity, and self-assertion. In his last novel, *Wilhelm Meisters Wanderjahre,* Goethe celebrated renunciation, contemplation, and the values of the group; the reader must strike a balance. *Faust* remains the expression of a splendid faith in man. It must be aligned with works like Lessing's *Nathan the Wise,* Mozart's *The Magic Flute,* Schiller's "Hymn to Joy," and Beethoven's Ninth Symphony, as the statement of the finest optimism of the eighteenth century, a pro-found, not a shallow belief. Yet in our time of troubles, it is an op-timism which we admire and perhaps envy; we can hardly accept it completely.

Mann

Our contemporary Thomas Mann has returned, with a vengeance, to the tragic view of Faust. His novel *Doctor Faustus* (1947) may even be viewed as a "taking back" of Goethe's *Faust;* he returns to the original legend, telling in a highly elaborate fashion of the damna-tion of a great modern musician, Adrian Leverkuehn, and of the German nation as a whole. In the novel, the account of the rise, decline, and fall of modern Germany is developed, parallel to that of the composer's career: we are never allowed to forget that this is the story of a nation as well as of an individual. Having experienced the Hitler regime, Mann was aware that a whole nation could sell its soul. Moreover, he became convinced that traits of spiritual ar-rogance, coldness, and "irrationalism," extending far back into the German cultural heritage, were coresponsible; it was not a matter of the Nazis alone. The German intellectuals as a group had been puffed up with pride and fascinated by evil.

Unfortunately for our purposes, Mann has complicated matters by exploring at the same time a very different theme: that of the "late" artist who comes upon the historical scene at a time when it has become almost impossible to create spontaneously. Leverkuehn, though enormously gifted, seems doomed to sterility; his compositions, devoid of warmth, tend more and more to sheer parody. To break through to a new expressive style, Leverkuehn, whose name signifies "bold living," sells his soul to the devil. In fact, the notion of the "breakthrough"—the violent irruption into a new state of things —is central.

> Fundamentally there is only one problem in the world, and it has this name. How does one break through? How does one emerge into the open air? How does one burst the chrysalis and become a butterfly? [15]

Mann uses this concept to connect the various levels of his work. Germany, which developed late as a nation, tries to burst out of encirclement into world power; preFascist groups discuss breaking down the social structure and completely recasting it; Adrian considers breaking the wall separating him from other men, though he is too proud to make the attempt; and he hopes that a new music will some day penetrate the confines of a narrow public to reach the people as a whole. It will be observed that some of the desired "breakthroughs" represent legitimate, and even noble aims; others are sinister. This discrepancy is perhaps the fundamental defect of a fascinating and powerful book.

Leverkuehn's pact with the devil is caused then by his desire to cast off the burden of the past and set up a new order of artistic creation. To put it in proper perspective, we must briefly trace his life. A child of the most "Faustian" region of Germany, born not far from Wittenberg, Leverkuehn is marked, even as a youth, by great intellectual brilliance, pride, and a strikingly cool, reserved manner. He is of a fundamentally religious nature and at first takes up theology, but soon shifts to a musical career. His music is curiously cold, mocking, devoid of emotional content; and in his own life he remains in self-willed isolation. Given this situation and his towering ambition, he is fair game for the devil. A strange encounter, however, precedes the formal pact: Leverkuehn, who has lived in complete

---

[15] *Cf.* Thomas Mann, *Doctor Faustus*, translated by H. T. Lowe-Porter, Knopf, New York, 1948, pp. 307 f.

chastity up to this point, is irresistibly attracted by a prostitute and deliberately infects himself. Mann implies that he does so because he senses that the disease will heighten his powers, enabling him to create greatly, during periods of euphoria, and thus to "break through." Thus the embrace of the prostitute is the actual pact with the devil. The incident may seem more bizarre than credible; Mann has borrowed it from the life of Nietzsche, himself a very "Faustian" person, who is thought by some commentators [16] to have contracted syphilis deliberately.

In the exact center of the novel Mann has placed his *tour de force*, Leverkuehn's interview with the devil. It does not greatly matter whether we think of the tempter as literally present, in the twentieth century, or assume that he is projected by the diseased mind of Leverkuehn: the point is that he is real to the musician. No pact is signed—that would be redundant—but the conversation is of decisive significance. The devil argues that in a "late" age like our own spontaneous creativity is normally impossible: the artist must have illicit inspiration, must sell his soul. A man who has compacted with hell is forbidden to love: presumably this is the theological equivalent of Adrian's coldness and Luciferian pride. Above all, the devil states that future generations will draw health from Adrian's music: that the ultimate result of his disease will be magnificent and beneficent works of art. (Mann's devil, it must be stressed, is no liar.) Here lies the justification of Adrian's actions. Had he refused to sell his soul, he would have betrayed his own genius; his great works could never have been written.[17] Leverkuehn takes on the character of nobility, of self-sacrifice, of vicarious suffering.

After the climactic dialogue, events move with increasing speed. In Leverkuehn's life, periods of feverish creation alternate with times of miserable illness; the devil keeps his word, and great music is written. In the development of Germany, similarly, there are years of apparent recovery and hope, as in the time of the Weimar Republic, but the general direction is downward. Adrian, like the protagonist

---

[16] H. W. Brann, *Nietzsche und die Frauen*, Meiner, Leipzig, 1931, p. 208.

[17] Compare the paradox of the "fortunate fall": the notion that mankind gained, in the long run, by the transgression of Adam and Eve.

of the *Faustbook,* violates the devil's commands by trying to love and to repent: but his efforts only accelerate the catastrophe. In a final farewell to his friends, modeled after the *Faustbook,* he confesses all his sins, real and imagined, and then collapses into complete madness. Unlike Goethe's Faust, Adrian has paid in full for his offenses. The fictitious narrator links his end with the final defeat of the Third Reich, and concludes with a brief prayer: "God have mercy on your soul, my friend, my fatherland." The end seems to be utter destruction and complete darkness. Yet in his account of Adrian's last work, "The Lamentation of Dr. Faustus," the narrator notes the paradox that Leverkuehn's mathematically constructed music has here achieved sheer expressiveness—"expression as lament." He goes on to suggest a parallel religious paradox:

. . . may we not . . . say too (though only in the lowest whisper) that out of the sheerly irremediable, hope might germinate? It would be but a hope beyond hopelessness, the transcendence of despair—not its betrayal, but the miracle that passes belief.[18]

If the "hope beyond hopelessness" is remembered together with the devil's promise to Leverkuehn that his works will be part of some healthy future culture, it appears that the despairing historical pessimism of *Doctor Faustus* is not unrelieved. After an extreme of degradation, there may be a turn back to light. Adrian will clearly be justified by his works; his "damnation" as an individual is an expression, after all, of his condition as an artist: he has sacrificed his life for the sake of his music. Even for the German nation, which "sold its soul" in a far more decisive way than he did, a faint but definite hope appears.

Here, as in the other treatments of the Faust legend, a paradox appears: "selling one's soul" does not, to some of our authors, entail treason to one's self; it may symbolize something very different.[19] For the orthodox author of the original *Faustbook,* of course, there

[18] Mann, *op. cit.,* p. 491.

[19] In this connection, one thinks of a variant of the Faust legend, Chamisso's *Peter Schlemihl.* Schlemihl makes a pact with the devil to sell his shadow—that is, his reputation—but he valiantly rejects the temptation to buy it back at the cost of his soul.

could be no distinction between the two concepts. The condition of Marlowe's *Faustus* is tragic in the full sense: had he not entered into the compact, he would have been untrue to his finest qualities; yet having done so, he is damned. Goethe's Faust could have betrayed himself, as we have seen, only by denying his very essence, by relapsing into passivity. A Faust who stayed in his study, a Leverkuehn unwilling to pay any price to write his music—these would have truly sold their souls. "He who saves his life shall lose it." For Goethe and Mann, contracting with the devil seems to signify the willingness to live boldly and adventurously, if need be, sinfully, for the sake of some great aim. Both writers vindicate the choices made by their protagonists. Error and sin may be forgiven; a failure to live to the utmost of one's abilities would be the unforgivable, indeed the inconceivable, "great refusal." This may be called a romantic view of life, no doubt. In any case, it is a view which is central to Goethe's *Faust,* as it is to Mann's.

IX

THE DILEMMA OF HAMLET

(William Shakespeare: *Hamlet*)

BY

EDGAR JOHNSON

I

Hamlet is a play and Hamlet is a character in that play. In exploring our topic, "The Dilemma of Hamlet," although the problem of the play and the problem of the man are tightly interknit, it is important for us to keep clearly in mind when we are talking about the one and when about the other.

My thesis about the play is that its leading theme is the relationship of appearance and reality—that its dilemma, or the series of dilemmas it poses for us, so to speak, is the difficulty of distinguishing between the actuality and the plausible appearance of wisdom or virtue or right action. This note is struck almost at the beginning, with Hamlet's acid, "I know not 'seems,'" and his hatred of hypocrisy and deception, coming hard upon his own distrustful and evasive answers to Horatius and Marcellus after speaking with his father's ghost, and followed immediately by his assumption of an "antic disposition" apparently designed to deceive Claudius and the Court into believing him insane, but leaving the spectator as well sometimes uncertain whether Hamlet's madness is assumed or whether his reason is breaking down under inward emotional strain. Madness and sanity, true wisdom and corruptly shrewd worldliness, real kingly leadership and tricky opportunism, genuine heroism and its showy counterfeit; these are some of the distinctions the play challenges us to make. But they lead us to Hamlet the man, about whom my thesis—partly paralleling that of G. R. Elliott—is that his dilemma is not only to bring about justice but to do so in a right frame of mind and feeling, acting as the scourge and minister of heavenly justice, not poisoned in soul by vengefulness and hatred.

In order to test these two theses and explore the dilemmas they deal with, we must glance at what Hamlet himself is like and what happens in the drama that bears his name. It might seem at first that this is simply done, merely by reading the play or seeing it performed. But history shows an extraordinary chaos of voices offering confused and contradictory explanations of both.

First, there is what may almost be called the orthodox version of the past one hundred and fifty years, the romantic interpretation that sees the young Prince Hamlet as an introvert entangled in hesitating thought to the point where he is frustrated to follow any course of action. This is the view of Hamlet's character most early and most eloquently voiced by Goethe and Coleridge. "A lonely, pure, noble and most moral character, without the strength of nerve that forms the hero," Goethe says of Hamlet, "sinks beneath the burden which it cannot bear and must not cast away. Impossibilities are required of him; not in themselves impossibilities, but such for him. He winds, and turns, and torments himself; he advances and recoils; is ever put in mind, ever puts himself in mind; at last does all but lose his purpose from his thoughts; yet still without recovering his peace of mind."

This description seems to imply that Shakespeare's hero was a fusion of Goethe's own Werther and Wilhelm Meister; Coleridge paid Hamlet the compliment of assuming that Shakespeare had been painting a sixteenth century version of the nineteenth century Coleridge. "He intended," wrote Coleridge, "to portray a person in whose view the external world and all its incidents and objects, were comparatively dim and of no interest in themselves, and which began to interest only when they were reflected in the mirror of his mind. . . . [Hamlet indulges in] endless reasoning and hesitating—constant urgency and solicitation of the mind to act, and as constant an escape from action; ceaseless reproaches of himself for sloth and negligence, while the whole energy of his resolution evaporates in these reproaches. This, too, not from cowardice, for he is drawn as one of the bravest of his time—not from want of forethought or slowness of apprehension, for he sees through the very souls of those who surround him; but merely from that aversion to action which prevails among such as have a world in themselves."

Such a view of Hamlet is on the whole accepted by Bradley and E. K. Chambers, and is essentially that of Laurence Olivier's film version of the play, where, in the beginning, while ghostly mists swirl around the battlements and cold vaulted interiors of Elsinore, a disembodied voice intones, "This is the tragedy of a man who could not make up his mind."

Opposed to this judgment is the approach of those like Kittredge, who see Hamlet as a man of action moving to avenge his father's death with no essential hesitation and all practicable dispatch, his self-reproaches caused only by chafing at the slowness imposed upon him by circumstances. This Hamlet demands, in conscience, to be sure, reasonable certitude that he has not been deceived by a lying phantom. When he has that assurance, in the King's guilty reaction to the play-within-the-play, he is still delayed by the difficulty of producing objective proof, convincing to the world, that he has not simply invented an accusation to justify regicide and a merely ambitious desire to seize the throne. This view argues, furthermore, that as a King, Claudius—except on the one accidental occasion when Hamlet comes on him at his prayers—is constantly surrounded by armed courtiers and attendants and even a corps of Swiss mercenaries; and after Hamlet has put him on his guard by showing that his crime is known, he not only takes steps for his own safety by sending Hamlet off to what he hopes will be the nephew's death in England, but would not be likely to let Hamlet approach him thenceforth without being surrounded by protection. In the culminating duel scene, it is only the conspiracy between Claudius and Laertes to kill Hamlet that allows him to be in the King's presence armed— and even then only in consequence of seizing Laertes's foil, the single one with an unbated point.

J. Dover Wilson, in turn, takes issue with a part of this argument by insisting that Hamlet never wanted to prove to the *world* that Claudius was his father's murderer. Such a view would always leave at least a stain of suspicion that Queen Gertrude was implicated, and, indeed, until after the play scene, in the interview in his mother's closet, Hamlet himself is by no means certain that she has not been privy to his father's death. But the ghost has bade Hamlet leave her to heaven, and therefore Hamlet has with great ingenuity, Wilson argues, devised the play to show *Claudius* that his guilt is known, but at the same time to make it appear to the scandalized court that it embodies his own threat to murder the present King. (Hamlet himself, you will recall, identifies the murderer in the play as *nephew* to the King.)

W. W. Greg has devised a still more radical overturn of previous themes. For him, the reason Claudius fails to be alarmed by the dumbshow of the murder, but breaks up the performance of the play, is that he is in fact innocent. He has not recognized the dumb-show as directed against himself, but does, with the court, take the subsequent action of the play as prefiguring an attempt on his own life. The ghost's accusations, heard by no one but Hamlet, are simply a hallucinating projection of his own deluded suspicions and have no basis in fact. Hamlet is in truth even madder than he has been pretending to be.

T. S. Eliot concludes that none of these explanations will really do. More, Hamlet's self-disgust and his revulsion at his mother's adultery and what Hamlet calls her incest, the nauseated loathing with which his imagination dwells in revolted detail upon "The bloat King" "honeying and making love" to his mother "in the rank sweat of an enseamed bed" "over the nasty stye," seem to Eliot emotions so excessive for the facts that he regards them as insufficiently motivated in the drama, and drawn from some hidden source in Shakespeare himself. "*Hamlet,*" he says, ". . . is full of some stuff that the writer could not drag to light, contemplate, or manipulate into art." Consequently, "So far from being Shakespeare's masterpiece, the play is certainly a failure."

At this point, generations of theatergoers who have regarded Hamlet with absorbed sympathy and no conscious puzzlement whatever might well feel tempted to exclaim in the witty words of one Shake-spearean commentator, "Are the critics of *Hamlet* mad or only pretending to be?" We seem to be in Spenser's wandering wood in which the thousands of paths lead only to Error's Den. But there is one more, with which I shall bring this survey of the critics to a conclusion, the psychoanalytic theory originally propounded by Freud and elaborated by Ernest Jones.

According to this, Hamlet is suffering from what he cannot possibly recognize himself, the Oedipal desire of a son to kill his father and supplant him in his mother's love. Only so, Jones claims, can we explain Hamlet speaking to her like a jealous lover, torturing himself with hideous images of her lovemaking, and hating the King with all the hysterical loathing of a rival. But because Claudius has done only what Hamlet himself desired to do, killed the father and mated with the mother, Hamlet partly identifies himself with his uncle, shares his guilt, and cannot bring himself to execute vengeance on one who has put into action what he himself dreamed in childhood fantasy. He consequently oscillates, between his conscious and acquired adult devotion to his father and his infantile hatred and aggression, and is inhibited from acting upon either. He would never be able to act effectively on either of his divided motives, and only accident brings the play to a catastrophic ending as fatal to himself as to Claudius.

II

The refutation of the argument is essential in my position, for if Jones is right, there *is* no moral dilemma in the drama. By definition Hamlet *cannot* understand his difficulty; only if—what is impossible —we could bring a twentieth century psychoanalyst to the imaginary twelfth century court of Elsinore as described by the sixteenth century dramatist, could Hamlet be taught to resolve his own confusions and solve his problems. Such an objection, of course, does not dispose of Jones's theory, nor does any mere skepticism about Shakespeare having thus foreshadowed a Freudian case history. Only if there are within the play itself and its effect upon a fit audience elements that do not square with this explanation, may we set aside it or the Goethe-Coleridge interpretation of which it is a more scientificsounding variant. And in the same way, to deal with any of the interpretations we have surveyed, we must look to the play and the impression it must produce on an audience that responds to it in the way molded by the dramatist.

But there are such elements to negate many of these interpretations. It is a minor caveat, no doubt, to object that the interview between mother and son in the Queen's closet, with Polonius hiding behind the arras, does not take place in her bedroom, as Freud and Jones say, with Hamlet violently flinging her upon the bed in the way Olivier does in the film. In Shakespeare's day, a closet was a small private room or study; Queen Gertrude would no more receive Polonius in her bedroom than Queen Elizabeth II would Winston Churchill. But (what is more fatal for the entire Jones-Freud-Coleridge-Goethe theory) Hamlet has not, before the opening of the play, been at all a frustrated introvert entangled in morbid thought and incapable of action, nor, as I shall show, does he really—except in certain very limited respects—show himself inactive in the course of the play.

It is true that with his father's death he has been plunged into the deepest grief and melancholy and that his mother's hasty marriage has filled him with horror and revulsion. Hamlet does indeed bear within him a misery "that passes show," and feels that the earth is "a sterile promontory," the heavens "a pestilent congregation of vapors," man a "quintessence of the dust." But it is important to note that the world *had not* been so for him; it had been a "goodly frame," the heavens a "majestical roof fretted with golden fire," and man "the beauty of the world," "the paragon of animals." In saying he has lost his mirth and foregone all customary exercise, he reveals that melancholy and inactivity had not been his habits when his father lived (of whom, according to Jones, he was no less secretly jealous than he now is of his uncle). But even now, throughout his present distresses, he *does* exercise, and has even moments of highspirited jesting. Before he becomes suspicious that Rosencrantz and Guildenstern are spying emissaries of the King, his greeting of them is gay rather than gloomy; and we learn later that he has been practising fencing daily all the while Laertes has been in France, and see Hamlet easily outmatch that skilled swordsman.

Others in the play testify not only to his multitudinous and shining accomplishments, but to his ease, grace, and charm. "The courtier's, soldier's, scholar's, eye, tongue, sword; The expectancy and rose of the fair state; The glass of fashion and the mold of form, the observed of all observers," Ophelia says of him. These are not the words in which one would describe a melancholy moper, who could not take the place of brilliant leadership at court to which his rank entitled him. When he is dead, Fortinbras, decreeing him a soldier's burial, summarizes general report in the valediction that "he was likely to have proved most royally." Are these the things others would say of an ineffectual dreamer?

Hamlet's behavior during the course of the play, furthermore, reveals none of the inwardturned embarrassment in social relations that characterize the introvert. He talks readily and cordially with soldiers, actors, gravediggers, gets along well with pirates, and is so beloved by the common people that Claudius dares not openly harm him, the last a popularity that introverts have seldom enjoyed with the populace. He easily takes command of any conversation in which he participates, usually with unassuming courtesy; and in the play scene he dominates the whole court. He is *not* hesitant or inhibited in action, even against Claudius; he plans the play to test the King's conscience in a flash, and carries it out flawlessly; he stabs Polonius through the arras more than half suspecting it to be the King (what of the notion that he *cannot* act against Claudius?); he sends the traitorous Rosencrantz and Guildenstern to their deaths instantly and without a qualm; he leaps on board the pirate ship before any can follow him; he accepts Laertes's challenge without a moment's pause; he sends Claudius a letter announcing himself landed naked in his Kingdom, as it were warning Claudius of his intentions; and he calmly plans to use the period before news can arrive from England to finish his task.

Jones argues that Hamlet's "mother fixation" stands between him and his courtship of Ophelia, but it does nothing of the kind. He has written her letters so ardent that Laertes warns her not to be moved by them, and won her with "words of so sweet breath composed," she herself says, "as made [his gifts] more rich." He has not drawn back from her; it is she, obedient to her father's command, not of her own will, who has repulsed him. Where in all this is the self-frustrated lover?

Given Hamlet's intense but not at all abnormal devotion to his father, is there anything excessive in his disgust at his mother's conduct? In any society except that of second century Rome, Hollywood, or the fast set of a modern cosmopolitan city, a son might well be shocked at his mother's adultery. And for an Elizabethan audience there was no question that her marriage to Claudius was incest as well. When Henry VIII married his elder brother's widow, Catherine of Aragon, in 1509, it was necessary to support a dispensation permitting it by bringing forward testimony that her previous marriage had never been consummated, and the feeling of horror that such a wedding violated biblical law endured long past Shakespeare's day. Hamlet only gives eloquent voice to an emotion all sixteenth century audiences understood.

Finally, there is the allegation that Hamlet delays unconscionably, unintelligibly, and fatally in executing justice upon Claudius. One might ask why it is no sign of Claudius's having some Freudian complex that he delays, no less fatally for himself, to kill Hamlet, long after he has realized that his nephew is dangerous. But the truth is that neither is dilatory except for quite intelligible reasons. It was entirely clear to an Elizabethan audience that a ghost might be a lying spirit and that a Prince intent on acting justly must prove its accusations, however strongly he felt impelled to believe them. The events of Acts II and III, and the first half of Act IV, all take place in a single day and night, and that day is so short a time after Polonius has forbidden Ophelia to see Hamlet, that only then has Hamlet become aware that her avoidance of him is deliberate and made his way into her chamber. The very next day the players come to Elsinore, Hamlet forms his plan, and puts it into effect. After he has lost his one chance to kill the King at prayer, he is packed off to England under guard. The intervening time is only long enough to bring Laertes back from Paris and permit Hamlet to land from the pirate ship. Hamlet can hardly slay Claudius during Ophelia's burial, on sacred ground, but he knows he has until messages arrive from England, coolly plans to use that interim, and, when he finds himself poisoned, kills the King an instant later. What an indecisive, will-less jack-o'-dreams!

In thus analyzing the Freudian interpretation, I have also dealt implicitly with most of the others I outlined in the first third of this paper, but I should still say a few words about Greg's theory that Claudius is innocent and Hamlet suffering from delusions. Dover Wilson's suggestion that during the dumbshow Claudius is discussing with Polonius the renewed display Hamlet has just given them of love-madness, and consequently has not observed the pantomime, in my opinion, partly answers Greg, but he is fully refuted by Claudius's own soliloquy in the prayer scene where the King explicitly admits "the primal curse" of "a brother's murder." This is unanswerable and we need say no more of it.

III

There remains only to sketch in such aspects of my own position as have not been anticipated in the previous part of the discussion. The theme of the play, I have said, is the relationship of appearance and reality, the gradual classification of moral identities deliberately portrayed ambiguously in the beginning. "Something is rotten in the State of Denmark," says Marcellus, and Hamlet cries out that it is "an unweeded garden," lamenting "the time is out of joint: Oh cursed sprite, that ever I was born to set it right." But we do not know at this point lest perhaps it is Hamlet himself who is the canker in the State, proud, revengeful, consumed with frustrated ambition to ascend the throne himself and rationalizing his fury at having been passed over in the election. (We might note that, like Hamlet, Fortinbras has failed to secure *his* father's throne, which is likewise now occupied by an uncle, but that unlike Hamlet he seems to feel no sense of injustice in this; he is more concerned to win back the half of Norway his father lost to the elder Hamlet.)

During the opening scenes of the play, I must reemphasize the point, we do not *know* whether Hamlet or Claudius is in the right. Let us try to imagine seeing or reading it for the first time, without having heard anything about it. Can we tell with certainty that Hamlet's jealousies and suspicions are true in fact? The original Hamlet story in *Saxo Grammaticus* was a pure revenge drama, with small moral cause to prefer the murdered King to his fratricide brother; and Hamlet's motives are entirely those of filial partisanship demanding an eye for an eye, a tooth for a tooth, not those of horror at a noble and virtuous King done to death by an evil one. Not, of course, that the Elizabethan audience before whom Shakespeare's play was first acted was likely to have known anything about *Saxo Grammaticus,* but the earlier Hamlet play of the 1590's, from which Shakespeare probably derived his own, also seems in turn to have been derived from *Saxo Grammaticus* and possibly Belleforest, and to have been straight melodrama, with a ghost crying "Hamlet, revenge!" Elizabethan playgoers may well have been surprised by the turn Shakespeare gave the old materials. From neither the opening of *Hamlet* nor its title have we any more assurance that Hamlet will be justified in its sequel than we have of Julius Caesar being the hero or Macbeth the villain of the Shakespearean plays that bear their names.

In the same way, we have in the pseudokingly Claudius, at first, a deceptively persuasive imitation of genuine kingliness: dignity, courtesy, affability, vigorous and effective diplomatic and military action against external danger, an eloquent and seemingly sincere statement of sound principles, both of feeling and of conduct. It is possible, for all we know at the moment, that Hamlet may indeed be giving way to a too protracted, unmanly, and self-indulgent grief in which he evades his duty to himself and to others. There is even a real regard for Hamlet in Claudius at first, a genuine kindness and good feeling, and there is no question of his affection for his Queen. Even when by degrees we pierce beneath his smiling mask, we find that he still struggles with conscience, that his slowness to act against his dangerous nephew is not all policy, and that only after his situation has grown desperate is conscience strangled.

With the old councillor Polonius, we have an impressive appearance of wise understanding and justice of judgment gradually yielding to vanity, worldliness, and senility. When he bids Laertes be faithful in friendship, and tells him "To thy own self be true," his morality sounds like that of Socrates, but the rest of his maxims are all prudential and concerned with the figure a man cuts in the world, rather than with essence—like his advice on money and on dress, a mere cautiousness of conduct or of taste. As the action proceeds, he sinks lower, and we see him willing to dispatch spies and informers upon his own son, eavesdropping and spying himself, flattering and hypocritical, obstinately determined to prove his own theories, a conceited busybody foolishly self-deceived.

Laertes is the pseudoheroic as Claudius is the pseudokingly. How gallant a figure he seems at first, how earnest is his concern for his sister, how admirable his promptness of action in demanding an explanation of his father's death (strikingly contrasted with Hamlet's seeming—though only seeming—slowness). But then, in more significant contrast to Hamlet's insistence on having proof and acting in right conscience, see Laertes storming into the King's presence, shouting before he knows the facts, "Conscience and grace to the profoundest pit," "To hell allegiance," and follow how easily the smooth King not merely deludes him but works him to a weak participation in villainy. Laertes, like his father, is concerned with appearance, not reality; he wants "formal ostentation" of funeral rites for Polonius and is concerned lest the world think he has not done enough. "What ceremony else?" he demands at Ophelia's grave, and his showy sorrow revolts Hamlet's inward grief "which passes show."

But Hamlet, the hero, too, is not all heroic, or only gradually becomes so. His wit is fiercely intolerant of stupidity and sycophancy; he is mockingly contemptuous of the affected Osric. He is consistently and publicly rude to Claudius, even before he knows the ghost's accusations; he is indecently discourteous, almost invariably, in deriding Polonius, whose daughter he loves; he is brutally harsh to his mother. Until well on in his plans, he is mistrustful of the sane and truehearted Horatio, refusing to confide in him, seeking neither the comfort nor the good counsel of a faithful friend, but bottling all his feelings and his purposes up within his breast, in a proud and suspicious secrecy. He is insultingly suspicious of Ophelia, leaping from the realization that her pathetic attempt to return his gifts means that their encounter is no accident, as it was meant to seem, to the raging conviction that she is her father's willing tool conniving to betray him. With furious bitterness he all but calls her a whore, and, despite the likelihood that spies are listening, recklessly shouts, "We'll have no more marriages. Those that are married already, all but one, shall live." Worst of all, for more than half the play, his determination to avenge his father's murder is a ferocious, hysterical, vindictive, bloody hatred that he can hardly keep within bounds. It is revenge with hardly a trace of concern for any nobler concept of justice.

This is the dilemma of Hamlet the Prince and Man—to disentangle himself from the temptation to wreak justice for the wrong reasons and in evil passion, and to do what he must do at last for the pure sake of justice, for the welfare of the State, to weed the unweeded garden of Denmark and set right the time that is out of joint. From that dilemma of wrong feelings and right actions he ultimately emerges, solving the problem by attaining a proper state of mind. At the end of the play scene, it is true, he refuses to kill Claudius at prayer, and excuses that evasion to himself by arguing that he wants to damn his uncle's soul more deep in hell by taking him at some time that has no relish of grace or salvation in it. But there is no improbability in suggesting that Hamlet is trying here to excuse a reluctance he does not yet understand but that springs from a revolt of his own conscience against acting with such poisonous feeling. He is acting—or rather refraining—on right motives, but giving himself mistaken reasons. (It is a dramatic irony of course, that Claudius has been unable to pray with sincerity, and is *not* in a state of grace.)

Slowly, however, in the course of the last two acts, Hamlet subdues his violence of feeling. Even by the end of the interview in his mother's closet, he sorrows for his impetuous murder of Polonius: "For this same Lord," he says, "I do repent"; and he gently bids his mother good night, telling her, "When you are desirous to be blest, I'll blessing beg of you." He prays Laertes's pardon for the wrong he has done him, and throughout all the ending moderates even those wild and whirling words of hatred he has previously spoken against

Claudius. Instead he asks, calmly, "Is't not perfect conscience to quit him with this arm?" and prevent "This canker of our nature" from proliferating "further evil." He has resolved the moral dilemma of vengeance *versus* justice. (Although it is true that when he has transfixed the King with Laertes's "envenomed point" he has a last spasm of hatred for the "incestuous, murderous, damnęd Dane.") At the end, Hamlet is even able to think of providing for a peaceful succession to the crown by giving his dying voice to Fortinbras. He expires with noble serenity, "The rest is silence." He has purged his nature of its fierce passions and become the great and heroic figure we always felt struggling in him to be born. As restoring peace descends over troubled Denmark, we can echo Horatio:

> "Good night, sweet prince,
> And flights of angels sing thee to thy rest!"

X

THE CHOICE OF SOCRATES

(Plato: *Crito*)

BY

RICHARD McKEON

The final choice of Socrates, which brought his life to its close, was the consequence, logical as well as historical, of the choices and decisions which made up his life. He refused to use the means provided by his friends for escape and for life in exile, and chose instead to remain in prison and undergo the death sentence imposed by his fellow citizens. The Socratic irony was not merely a rhetorical figure employed in argument; it was a quality of Socrates's life: the refusal to save his life at the cost of abandoning values followed as consequence from the opposition he demonstrated between good and advantage-seeking and from his repeated judgment that it is better to suffer than to do evil. In his defense, as recorded in Plato's *Apology,* Socrates enumerated for his judges the final paradoxes of his choice: the issue of the trial was an accusation brought against a man for doing good; the penalty, death, which the defendant did not fear because it could not harm him, could have been avoided if he performed actions which would harm him—if he acquiesced in statements that were false and unjust, or corrupt and adapted to the prejudices of his judges; the final judgment was to bring punishment to the judges, not to the condemned. The paradoxes are the ideals of Socrates developed in dialectical statement. It would be difficult to separate the inspiration of his example from the irritation of his arguments in the history of Western culture. His influence after his death, and the effects which his successors have been inspired to trace back to him, have been as paradoxical as his life.

This man, condemned and executed by due process of law or by a miscarriage of justice, for impiety and for corrupting the morals of the young, has been celebrated for piety and for doubt; he has been the progenitor of idealisms and skepticisms; the beginnings of moral philosophy and the application of reason to practical problems have been traced to his inquiries, and he has been accused of separating philosophy from life and of initiating the tradition of vacuous academic philosophy; he has been praised as the pioneer of scientific method and logic and has been lumped with the Sophists and criticized for verbal trickery; his example has been invoked by skeptics and dogmatists, pragmatists and speculatives, rationalists and mystics, who have all professed to use the Socratic method and attitude. He has been criticized for separating knowledge from eloquence, for confusing argument with sophistry, for reducing theory to practice, and for dissociating reason and the passions. His paradoxes have been exemplified in most of the issues of knowledge and action that men have pondered since his time, frequently under the influence of ideas that are traced back to conversations he initiated. His choice is at the center of the moral and political dilemmas of our times.

The paradoxes of the life and influence of Socrates cannot be stated in simple form since the histories in which his career has been recounted are involved in like paradoxes. Historians have chosen, in continuous circle, both of the contradictory interpretations which the evidence can be made to support. Either the Athenians repented immediately after the death of Socrates and justice was done, somewhat tardily, by vindicating his memory and by punishing his accusers; or, the friends and disciples of Socrates, in their apologies, memoirs, and dialogues, combatted a dominant hostile or unsympathetic view, and their surviving writings are taken as evidence, since the case for the prosecution is preserved only in their refutations, of the facts of the case and of a general and considered favorable reaction to the facts. The first alternative is summarized eloquently by Diogenes Laertius:

So he was taken from among men; and not long afterward the Athenians felt such remorse that they shut up the training grounds and gymnasia. They banished the other accusers and put Meletus to death; they honored Socrates with a bronze statue, the work of Lysippus, which they placed in the hall of processions. And no sooner did Anytus visit Heraclea than the people of that town exiled him on the very day. . . . Euripides upbraids them thus in his *Palamedes:* "Ye have slain, have slain, the all wise, the innocent, the Muse's nightingale." This is one account; but Philochorus asserts that Euripides died before Socrates.[1]

Other anachronisms have slipped into the account, besides the one which Diogenes Laertius acknowledges, and the surviving evidence throws enough doubt on the reported repentance of the Athenians to lend plausibility to the second alternative. The case was debated long after the trial had come to its close and the decision of the judges had been executed, and the issue was extended inevitably from the defense of Socrates's reputation to the fuller elaboration of his ideas. Polycrates, the Sophist, seems to have prepared, shortly after the trial, an organized statement of the case of Anytus and Meletus; he is probably the "accuser" whom Xenophon answers in his *Memorabilia,* and some notion of his accusations can be reconstructed from the *Apology of Socrates* written by Libanius, a rhetorician of the fourth century A.D.—misuse of the poets to yield immoral interpretations, teaching disrespect for elders, the law, and the existing constitution, encouragement of neglect of civil duties coupled with advocacy of recourse to violence with results graphically exemplified in the careers of Alcibiades and Critias and in the overthrow of the democracy. The dialogues and *Memorabilia* of Xenophon are simple refutations of these charges; the few fragments that remain of the seven dialogues of Aeschines of Sphettus suggest a subtler personality and a more complex background of social forces; the dialogues of Plato present the defense of Socrates in a context of philosophic, as well as social issues, and relate the paradoxes of Socrates's career to the paradoxes of his philosophic teaching.

"Socratic dialogues" were produced in such numbers that Aristotle treats them with the mime as a separate literary form,[2] and the "Socratic schools" developed almost every conceivable philosophical

---

[1] Diogenes Laertius, *Lives of the Philosophers,* ii. 43–44.

[2] Aristotle, *Poetics,* I. 1447[b]9–16. *Cf.* Diogenes Laertius, iii. 37: "Aristotle remarks that the style of the dialogues [*sc.* of Plato] is half-way between poetry and prose."

tendency—cynicism and skepticism, hedonism and ethical intellectu-
alism, eristic logic-chopping and dogmatic idealism. Aristotle's own
pronouncements credit Socrates with examining the nature of definition and proof for the first time and with originating methodical
inquiry into moral questions, but they separate the Socratic philosophy
sharply from the Platonic doctrine of ideas and all like metaphysical
commitments. The later history of Socrates's influence oscillates between extremes at either side of Aristotle's moderate report—from
accounts of a skeptical method adapted to find arguments in support of any position or of a pragmatic method adapted to refute
verbal relativism and conventional prejudice, to accounts of a metaphysical explanation of a universe modeled on a starkly rational
pattern and therefore accessible to dialectic, or of an inspired vision
compounded of mystery and mathematics and accessible to myth,
enthusiasm, and proportions. Even the Platonic tradition moved
between similar extremes: the Middle and New Academies were
skeptical and calculated practical probabilities; the New Platonism
was mystical and grounded dialectical arguments in metaphysical
emanations.

The paradoxes of a philosophy in which wisdom is ignorance and
self-knowledge, and virtue is knowledge or, in the absence of certifi-
able knowledge, "right opinion" motivated by *eros,* underlie the
paradoxes of Socrates's career and character. The philosophy of Socrates cannot be stated in theoretic or technical terms, nor can it be
stated without considering the systematic consequences which involved his disciples for over twenty centuries in the warfare of opposed schools. Socrates talked about philosophy and common issues,
and made no distinction between them. He talked about philosophy
with any one who was interested to examine what his own statements and beliefs meant, with philosophers and common men, with
statesmen, artisans, poets, rhetoricians, interpreters of poetry and
students of oratory, young men concerned with friendship, justice,
and beauty, old men interested in courage, the teaching of political
virtue, and the study of mathematics. Yet his defenders who gave
evidence against the charges of immoral influence or endangering
the state could not agree about his method and did not always dis-

tinguish it from Sophistic;[3] and a large and representative Athenian jury sentenced him to death on an issue of justice. He was an eloquent man, whose eloquence as he himself remarks ironically was inseparable from his philosophy,[4] redoubted in argument and more than the equal of the most skilled rhetorician. He was a wise man whose wisdom consisted in his recognition of his own ignorance.[5] Yet he lost his own case, not through lack of words to move his judges, but because of impudence and shamelessness in refusing to adapt his words to their preconceptions.[6] In the literature which has recorded and reviewed his argument and their judgment, he has usually been pronounced not only innocent but a paragon of virtue, and the immediate effect of his influence was to separate philosophy and rhetoric and to divide philosophy into schools.

Cicero who professed to be a follower of the skepticism of the New Academy, counts Socrates the parent and the prince of philosophy,[7] the originator of the practical applications of philosophy to life,[8] and the inventor of the method, constructed to oppose the

---

[3] Cf. *Aeschines*, i. 173: "You have put Socrates the Sophist to death, because he was shown to have educated Critias."

[4] Plato, *Apology*, 17A–18A.

[5] *Ibid.*, 20D–23B.

[6] *Ibid.*, 38D.

[7] Cicero, *De Finibus*, ii. 1. 1: *"parens philosophiae"*; *De Natura Deorum*, i. 34. 93: *"parens philosophiae"*; *ibid.*, ii. 66. 167: *"princeps philosophiae"*; *De Oratore*, i. 10. 42: *"fons et caput"* of the *"greges philosophorum."*

[8] *Tusculan Disputations*, v. 4. 10–11: "Socrates on the other hand was the first to call philosophy down from the heavens and set her in the cities of men and bring her also into their homes and compel her to ask questions about life and morality and things good and evil: and his many-sided method of discussion and the varied nature of its subjects and the greatness of his genius, which have been immortalized in Plato's literary masterpieces, have produced many warring philosophic sects of which I have chosen particularly to follow that one which I think agreeable to the practice of Socrates, in trying to conceal my own private opinion, to relieve others from deception and in every discussion to look for the most probable solution . . ." Cf. *De Legibus*, i. 12. 33–34: "Consequently Socrates was right when he cursed, as he often did, the man who first separated utility from justice, for this separation, he complained is the source of all mischief." Cf. also, Diogenes Laertius, ii. 21: "Demetrius of Byzantium relates that Crito removed him from his workshop and educated him, being struck by his beauty of soul; that he discussed moral questions in the workshops and the market-place, being convinced that the study of nature is no concern of ours; and that he claimed that his inquiries embraced 'Whatso'er is good or evil in a house'

eristic of the Sophists, which examined the grounds of all opinions and which was revived in the skepticism of the Academy.[9] The philosophers of all schools who speak in Cicero's dialogues had no doubt of Socrates's innocence [10] or of his piety. Cotta, the Academic, in the midst of his refutation of the Stoic view of divine providence on the grounds that the misfortunes of the good and the triumphs of the

---

[Homer, *Odyssey,* iv. 392]; that frequently, owing to his vehemence in argument, men set upon him with their fists or tore his hair out; and that for the most part he was despised and laughed at, yet bore all this ill-usage patiently."

[9] *Cf. De Finibus,* ii. 1. 1–2, where the method of Socrates, "who is entitled to be styled the parent of philosophy" is expounded in opposition to the method of the Sophists: "His own way was to question his interlocutors and by a process of cross-examination to elicit their opinions, so that he might express his own views by way of rejoinder to their answers. This practice was abandoned by his successors, but was afterwards revived by Arcesilas, who made it a rule that those who wished to hear him should state their own opinions; and when they had done so he argued against them." *Cf. Academica,* i. 4. 16: "The method of discussion pursued by Socrates in almost all the dialogues so diversely and so fully recorded by his hearers is to affirm nothing himself except the fact of his own ignorance, and that he surpassed all other people in that they think they know things that they do not know but he himself thinks he knows nothing, and that he believed this to have been the reason why Apollo declared him to be the wisest of all men, because all wisdom consists solely in not thinking that you know what you do not know. He used to say this regularly, and remained firm in this opinion, yet nevertheless the whole of his discourses were spent in praising virtue and in exhorting mankind to the zealous pursuit of virtue, as can be gathered from the books of members of the Socratic school, and particularly from those of Plato." *Cf. Brutus,* 7. 31: "Opposed to them [*sc.* the Sophists] was Socrates, who with characteristic adroitness of argumentation made it a practice to refute their doctrines. Out of the wealth of his discourses there emerged a group of men of great learning, and to them is attributed the first discovery of the philosophy which deals with good and evil, with human life and society, as distinguished from the philosophy of nature, which belonged to an earlier time."

[10] *Cf. De Oratore,* i. 54. 231: "Thus did a Roman of consular rank [*sc.* Publius Rutilius] follow the example of great Socrates of old who, as he was the wisest of all men, and had lived the most blameless of lives, defended himself in person, when indicted on a capital charge, in such fashion as to seem no submissive prisoner, but the teacher or master of his judges. Indeed, when Lysias, a most accomplished orator, brought him a written speech, to be committed to memory, if he thought proper, for use in his defense at his trial, he read it not unwillingly, and said it was aptly phrased: 'But,' he said, 'just as, if you had brought me a pair of Sicyonian half-boots, were they never so easy and well-fitting, I should reject them as womanish, even so I think your speech is skilful oratory but not the utterance of a brave man.' And so he too was condemned, not only at the first count, when the tribunal merely determined the issue of conviction or acquittal, but also on the further vote which they were bound by law to give."

wicked, the deaths of philosophers and the prosperity of tyrants, are evidence that the gods are indifferent to the fate of men, pauses to exclaim: "Why need I mention Socrates, whose death when I read Plato never fails to move me to tears?" [11] But although Socrates was the originator of philosophy, the inventor of a method suited to avoid dogmatism, and the first to turn philosophy to practical problems, his example had the effect of separating philosophy as a technical branch of study from eloquence and effective expression, and of dividing philosophers into warring schools and sects.

But as there have been certain persons and those a considerable number who either held a high position on account of their twofold wisdom, as men of action and as orators—two careers that are inseparable—, for instance Themistocles and Pericles and Theramenes, or other persons who were not themselves so much engaged in public life but were professional teachers of this same wisdom, for instance, Gorgias, Thrasymachus, Isocrates, persons have been found who being themselves copiously furnished with learning and talent, but yet shrinking on deliberate principle from politics and affairs, scouted and scorned this practice of oratory. The chief of these was Socrates, the person who on the evidence of all men of learning and the verdict of the whole of Greece, owing not only to his wisdom and penetration and charm and subtlety but also to his eloquence and variety and fertility easily came out on top whatever side in a debate he took up; and whereas the persons engaged in handling and pursuing and teaching the subjects that we are now investigating were designated by a single name, the whole study and practice of the liberal sciences (*omnis rerum optimarum cognitio atque in eis exercitatio*) being named philosophy, Socrates robbed them of this general designation, and in his discussions separated the science of wise thinking from that of elegant speaking, though in reality they are closely linked together; and the genius and varied discourses of Socrates have been immortally enshrined in the compositions of Plato, Socrates himself not having left a scrap of writing. This is the source from which has sprung the undoubtedly absurd and unprofitable and reprehensible severance between the tongue and the brain, leading to our having one set of professors to teach us to think and another to teach us to speak. For because of the plurality of schools that virtually sprang from Socrates, owing to the fact that out of his various and diverse discussions, ranging in every direction, one

[11] *De Natura Deorum*, iii. 32. 82.

pupil had picked up one doctrine and another another, there were engendered families at discord with one another and widely separated and unlike, although all philosophers claimed and sincerely claimed the title of followers of Socrates.[12]

The list of schools with which Cicero illustrates his thesis includes all the Hellenistic philosophic sects, except only the Epicurean—Platonic together with the various Academics, Peripatetic, Cynic, Stoic, Cyrenaic, Eretrian, Megarian, and Skeptic.

Knowledge of Socrates entered the Christian world on the double report of Plato and Cicero. Socrates was a saint and a skeptic, the father of philosophy and the source of the warring schools of philosophers, the first to engage in moral speculations and the originator of the method of professing ignorance or dissembling understanding in order to expose the errors of other doctrines. Justin Martyr numbered him with Abraham and the Hebrew Prophets among the ranks of Christians. St. Augustine repeated the account of his reform of philosophy, turning it from natural speculation to the practice of morality and the reformation of manners, of his method of disputation and his profession of ignorance, of his condemnation and death and the revulsion of the Athenians, and of the multiplication of schools—all as introduction to his account of the philosophy of Plato, who excelled all other philosophers and whose doctrines most nearly accorded with the truths of Christianity.[13] Christian philosophers learned from Augustine to refute the Academics and find the Platonic truths restated in their purity by Plotinus. During the Renaissance, when both Plato and Cicero were studied for the reform of philosophy and life, Socrates emerges in three guises: for Erasmus he becomes St. Socrates and his philosophy, merged with that of Plato, Cicero, and Seneca, is identified with Christian philosophy; for Montaigne he is a prototype of Pyrrhonian skepticism; for the Neoplatonists the analysis of love he learned from Diotima becomes part of the structure of the universe.

The developments of modern scholarship and modern philosophy have explored further implications of the old paradoxes. The careers

---

[12] *De Oratore*, iii. 16. 59–61.
[13] Augustine, *The City of God*, viii. 5.

of Socrates and Christ have been compared in a long series of books, and Socrates's contribution to the beginnings of philosophy and morals were reexamined both in relation to "preSocratic" philosophy and in relation to Platonic philosophy. In the dialectic of history, as Hegel constructs it, Socrates resolved the ambiguities of the relation of subjective and objective by expressing "real existence as the universal 'I,' as the consciousness which rests in itself," and he made the transition in ethics from objective or natural morality (*Sittlichkeit*) to subjective or reflective morality (*Moralitaet*); his condemnation, however, was just, for he set his conscience in opposition to the judges' sentence and the first principle of a State is that there is no reason or conscience or righteousness higher than what the State recognizes as such.[14] For Nietzsche, preSocratic thought, in the "Tragic Age of Greece," held Apollonian and Dionysian elements in union and balance, and the contribution of Socrates was to destroy that harmony and tension of rational and irrational, in the doubtful victory of the rational. The tragic view of life was made ethical and intellectual and reduced to dead pedantry. Schleiermacher, on the other hand, labored with the "Socratic Question," the search through the conflicting evidence of extant accounts for the "historical" Socrates: something more than Xenophon could appreciate, Schleiermacher argued, somewhat less than Plato suggests, along lines indicated by Aristotle's separation of the doctrine of ideas from Socrates's teaching. Zeller followed Schleiermacher and interpreted Socrates as a nonsystematic preparation for Plato, but more recently the testimony of Aristotle has been discredited again, and Socrates has become, according to Heinrich Maier, the creator of a new attitude toward life, the antitype of Christ and the Oriental religion of redemption, but not a theoretical philosopher like Plato, or he has been vindicated as a philosopher, according to John Burnet and A. E. Taylor, whose doctrines were precisely those Plato attributed to him, including the fundamental ideas from which metaphysics took its start. Philosophers likewise have again sought the authority of his

[14] Friedrich Wilhelm Nietzsche, *Hegel's Lectures on the History of Philosophy*, translated by E. S. Haldane, Routledge & Kegan Paul, London, 1955, vol. I, pp. 384–388, 442–443.

example and the use of his method in the service of a Christian, a utilitarian, a critical, a skeptical, a mystical, or a pragmatic philosophy.[15] But new reasons have also been found to justify the verdict of his judges. A. E. Taylor has argued that Socrates was, accord-

[15] Sören Kierkegaard, *Attack upon "Christendom,"* 1854–1855, translated by W. Lowrie, Princeton University Press, Princeton, 1944, p. 283: "The only analogy I have before me is Socrates. My task is a Socratic task, to revise the definition of what it is to be a Christian. For my part I do not call myself a 'Christian' (thus keeping the ideal free), but I am able to make it evident that the others are that still less than I." *Cf.* also *The Concept of Dread,* translated by W. Lowrie, Princeton University Press, Princeton, 1944, p. 99, n.: "Hence for one who is not thoroughly conversant with the Socratic method it proves disturbing that by Socrates the good, this apparently infinite abstraction, is instantly applied to the most concrete cases. The method is perfectly correct, except that he did amiss (to the Greek way of thinking he did rightly) in conceiving the good from its outward side (the useful, the finitely teleological)." Also *ibid.,* p. 120, "That it was Socrates who introduced irony into the world and gave the baby its name, that his irony was precisely the close reserve which began by shutting himself off from men, by shutting himself in with himself in order to be expanded in the Deity, began by shutting his door against men and making jest of those who stood outside, in order to talk in secrets—who troubles himself about that?" *Cf.* also, J. S. Mill, *Utilitarianism,* chap. 1. "And after more than two thousand years the same discussions continue, philosophers are still ranged under the same contending banners, and neither thinkers nor mankind at large seem nearer to being unanimous on the subject, than when the youth Socrates listened to the old Protagoras, and asserted (if Plato's dialogue be grounded on a real conversation) the theory of utilitarianism against the popular morality of the so-called sophist." *Cf.* also John Dewey, "William James' Morals and Julien Benda's: It is not Pragmatism that is Opportunist," *Commentary,* vol. VII, 1948, p. 49: "The ideological amalgam expressed in M. Benda's phrase, 'Socratic-Christian,' is, to say the least, perplexing. Socrates was put to death on the ground that his questioning of accepted moral and civic doctrines was subversive. According to all accounts, the one thing for which he stood, the one thing that caused his death at the hands of established and recognized authorities, was that he placed the right and authority of continued and systematic inquiry in the search for truth above all other authorities that claimed the right to regulate the course of life. M. Benda presumably has reasons he does not disclose for substituting 'Socratic-Christian' for the usual 'Judeo-Christian.' But as long as these reasons are kept occult, one can only say that it looks a good deal like an attempt to eat the cake of supernatural absolutism and at the same time keep some of it under the pretense of questioning absolute claims. In any case, it is pertinent to state that, on the face of known facts, those who still assert the right and authority of *critical* systematic examination of all *received* teachings and beliefs from any source—among whom pragmatists are numbered in the first rank—have the prior claim to the title 'followers' of Socrates." *Cf.* also *The Socratic: Contemporary Philosophy and Christian Faith. Papers by Contemporary Oxford Philosophers,* no. 1, with a Foreword by J. Wisdom, Philosophical Library, New York, 1952; Leonard Nelson, *Socratic Method and Critical Philosophy,* translated by Thomas K. Brown III, Yale University Press,

ing to law, actually guilty of the charge of impiety, since he was the center of an antidemocratic Pythagorean club, and therefore an adherent of a *religio non liciti*,[16] and the evidence Taylor adduces has been subtly transformed by Winspear and Silverberg to the Communist accusation that he had organized a conspiracy against the democratic constitution of Athens and an intellectual assault on the whole democratic way of life.[17]

Among all these paradoxes—historical, sociological, philosophical, theological, and cosmological—the moral-political paradoxes which Socrates explores in the *Crito* have particular pertinence to the problems men face today. The prior, and in a sense more fundamental, paradoxes have implications in the relation of thought and knowledge to practical crises, the relation of free inquiry to the doctrines established by inquiry and held by belief, and the relation of the community and the common good to the individual and his values. The basic paradoxes come to issue in the clash of irreconcilable actions in ethics and politics when moral criteria are sought to improve law and elevate custom, and the support and force of law are sought to give operation to moral codes and to preserve established values. These oppositions are in sharp focus in the fate of the man who sought to transcend the laws of his state in a wisdom by which it might have been improved and who refused to transgress the laws when they condemned him for the consequences of that effort. The career of Socrates suggests that these profound problems—together with the ambiguities of interpretation, imputation, and misrepresentation that complicate his treatment of them in theory and practice—are all implicated in the apparently simple problem of how a man can do his part in preserving democracy and in realizing the individual values which democracy should make practicable. We, too, live in disturbed and heroic times—many men, vastly more than were involved in all the wars and piety of ancient Athens, have faced the choice of death or exile, or simply the choice of attitude

New Haven, 1949; and R. Godel, *Socrate et le Sage Indien,* "Les Belles Lettres," Paris, 1953.

[16] A. E. Taylor, *Varia Socratica,* Parker, Oxford, 1911, pp. 27–30.

[17] Alban D. Winspear and Thomas Silverberg, *Who Was Socrates?* Gordon, Rahway, 1939, pp. 76–85.

under sentence of death, on charges of treason and disloyalty; and many more have faced the choice of silence or unpopularity. We are all involved in some form of the choice of Socrates, and if no presentday Socrates has emerged, that may be due to our disinclination or inability to face the paradoxes of our decisions or to the absence of a Plato capable of stating them. In the *Crito* the issues of the choice are discussed in terms of conflicts of loyalties familiar to all of us—self-interest, family, friends, and countrymen—and of a conception of justice which redefines self-interest and reinterprets the bonds of association.

Crito had come to Socrates's cell before dawn on the day before the return of the ship from Delos which was to mark the date of the execution of Socrates. He had plans for escape, as well as forceful reasons to persuade Socrates to acquiesce in them. People would criticize the friends of Socrates for failing to spend money or to take the trouble to secure his safety; he was taking the laziest way out; he was betraying himself and his children, whereas a good and brave man would act to frustrate his enemies and to assume the responsibilities he owed his family. Socrates urges, in reply, that they ought first to consider whether or not this course of action should be followed, and that they ought not be frightened by the penalties in the power of the multitude—imprisonment, death, and the confiscation of property—nor be guided by popular opinion. There is only one evil to be feared, wrongdoing, and only one judgment to be followed, that of the man who knows about just and unjust, good and bad, noble and disgraceful. The only question, therefore is, "Ought a man to do what he has agreed to do, provided it is right, or may he violate his agreements?" Socrates invokes the Laws and the Commonwealth themselves to state the argument against the action of one who would destroy the laws and his country. Their argument runs through the same loyalties and values which Crito had invoked: country is more revered and holier among gods and men of understanding than mother, father, and ancestors; the citizen owes all that he had to them, and all that he has may properly be taken away by them; to transgress the laws would do no good to friends or self— your friends would be subject to banishment and loss of property, and the laws of those who received you in exile would be endangered, while your own life would be emptied of justice and virtue, and even of conversations about them; you would be unable to give your children a proper education in exile and as a fugitive from justice; and even death would bring no surcease.

This is, as Socrates would say, a riddling answer to a question which was literally a choice between life and death. The arguments which Socrates puts in the mouth of the Laws and the State are, as he says, familiar—he has used them before and Crito has taken pleasure in them. They silence Crito now, but his final reply in the dialogue, "No, Socrates, I have nothing more to say," suggests that he is persuaded that he cannot convince Socrates rather than that Socrates has convinced him.

Crito was a "reasonable," "practical" man; and "intelligent" men would want to place the judgment of the Athenian people in its context rather than treat it in the frame of a myth removed from the contemporary reality that determines the fears and prejudices of people and the actions of courts. The year was 399 B. C. as we calculate chronology. The life of Socrates, now in his seventies, had coincided with the period of growth which had culminated in the great artistic, institutional, and intellectual achievements of the Age of Pericles and with the struggles by which the hegemony of Greece had passed from Athens to Sparta. Pericles himself had died thirty years earlier; the disasters of the Peloponnesian war had come to a fateful close five years before and had been followed by the Oligarchy of the Thirty Tyrants; Athens had spent the past four years beginning the slow process of rebuilding its power, influence, and self-respect in an atmosphere of widespread conviction that the disasters of the war were not unrelated to the tolerance accorded to the extravagances of intellectual crackpots—philosophers, poets, and Sophists—who were traitors to the state and who had flouted the traditional religion.

If Socrates had made an adaptation, in this atmosphere, of the arguments he developed against Crito's proposal, and had used those arguments as part of his defense at his trial, he would doubtless have influenced enough of the small majority by which he was condemned

—probably thirty votes, according to the evidence that has come to us—to secure acquittal. But instead of telling his judges that his philosophy led him to hold that the laws and his country were to be revered above every other attachment (even when they seemed on grounds of personal conviction to be wrong), he told them that he did not fear the death sentence which they had it in their lawful power to pass, because he had a higher allegiance to philosophy than to anything else in life, that he would not accept acquittal if the condition was that he abandon philosophy, for, much as he respected and loved them, he obeyed the god rather than a jury of Athenian citizens, who despite the reputation of Athens for wisdom and power esteemed the acquisition of wealth, reputation, and honor higher than wisdom, truth, and the perfection of the soul. Then he boasted that he twice refused to carry out the decrees of the government, once under the democracy and once under the oligarchy, because he thought them unjust. Yet now—as "intelligent" and "practical" men might properly argue—he abandons this argument in order to submit to a decision whose manifest injustice was a reaction to the attitude he displayed when he used it, because disobedience to the laws would destroy the foundations of the state.

This impatience, which practical men might feel, reflects a difficulty discovered by philosophers. In his arguments about virtue and statesmen, Socrates had been accustomed to seek the basis of the state in justice and truth by methods based on reason and wisdom: in the *Crito* the basis of the state is a compact or agreement in which citizens acquiesce simply by continuing residence in the state. His customary argument is a defense of the rights of the individual as defined by the law of nature and provides the means by which the state can progress and improve; it is abandoned, so the argument runs, for a defense of the right of a community to combat disorganizing and subverting influences. This paradox in the actions and arguments of Socrates is usually transformed into a paradox in the history on which its statement is based by raising questions concerning the accuracy of the Platonic account. It has been argued that the account is accurate, that the Socratic irony was expressed in this way in the career of Socrates, and that this is the issue which the Athenians faced. In this interpretation the history of the repentance of the Athenians and the swift justice they worked on Socrates's prosecutors are plausible. Or, it has been argued that the account is faithful to the facts alleged in the trial but not to Socrates's argument, and that the position that virtue is knowledge, which Socrates took in his discourses, is inconsistent with the role he assumes in the *Apology* as exhorter and preacher of virtue—and *a fortiori* with his role in the *Crito* as defender of law and order.[18] This interpretation is consistent with the hypothesis that the Athenian people did not in fact face this issue, since it was presented or invented by Plato and by the Socratics, and that it never entered into the deliberations of politicians or practical men but had its continuing life in the deliberations of philosophers and the enthusiasms of poets.

There is a third interpretation which might be put on the choice of Socrates which would draw its plausibility, if it were advanced, from the methods of the new criticism and the experience of the new propaganda. No one, today, would think of treating the philosophy of Plato or Aristotle (and the mode has been extended to other less systematic philosophers, even those concerning whom more biographical information is available) without taking into account the genetic evolution of their thought. Plato's last dialogue, the *Laws,* sets forth the organization of a state which departs in all essential respects from the impractical idealism of his more youthful *Republic.* It is a scheme, as one of the interlocutors in the dialogue puts it, practicable in an actual or secondbest state. The chief interlocutor is no longer Socrates, and his actual identity is masked in the anonymity of the "Athenian Stranger." Yet Aristotle, who was privy to the secrets of the Platonic Academy, attributes the arguments of the "Athenian Stranger" to Socrates.[19] Obviously, so the argument should run if it occurred to anyone to construct it, but in the welter of Socratic Questions it seems miraculously to have escaped attention, the friends of Socrates would not only have banded together to save their friend and master, but would also have taken shrewd measures

---

[18] Theodor Gomperz, *Greek Thinkers: A History of Ancient Philosophy,* translated by G. G. Berry, Scribner, New York, 1905, vol. II, pp. 104–118.

[19] *Politics,* ii. 6.

to cover his retreat, geographic and intellectual. Therefore, they would defend his career and philosophy by apologies and conceal his escape by arguing ironically, as Plato does in the *Crito,* that flight and exile would have been inconsistent with his philosophy and his integrity. Then after establishing the fiction that he had been executed, his friends could arrange to have Socrates return to Athens, in an anonymity as transparent as the understood fiction of his supposed death, to expound the more practical philosophy to which his experiences had brought him. An ingenious use of the methods of the new criticism would disclose many bits of evidence in the *Laws* to substantiate this hypothesis—and not the least would be the stringent regulations against impiety which the "Stranger" advocates for the new state.[20] The only miscarriage that can be traced back to this otherwise successful scheme is the trickery unwittingly practised on posterity which was deluded, since the common knowledge of the fictions employed was not set down in writing, into crediting the rhetorical defenses of the earlier Socrates at the expense of profiting by the philosophical enlightenment of the later—at least, until it is rediscovered by historical exercises in genetic criticism which justify abandoning what is said for what must obviously have been meant.

A paradox, in its simple sense, is a statement contrary to received opinion. Consequently it is apparently opposed to commonsense, although it may in fact be true or can be made to seem true. The paradoxes of Socrates, however, have to a high degree the virtue which has made the paradox an instrument of moral inspiration and reform and which is the continuing source of the Socratic "irony": they generate two sets of contradictory propositions, *either* of which may be espoused as the *common* opinion, and *both* of which can be shown to be false or, in a transformed higher sense, true. If virtue is knowledge, then it should be possible to teach virtue, and indeed all citizens are teachers of virtue, yet the sons of Pericles and other men who excelled in virtue received the best available education but were not taught virtue, and it would therefore seem that virtue is

[20] *Laws* x. 907C–910D. *Cf.* also *ibid.,* vii. 799B, x. 888A-D, and 899D ff.

right opinion, or inspiration, or love. If Socrates's wisdom was his ignorance, it would follow that he knew nothing and yet knew more than other men. And if he was guided by wisdom and his *daimon* in his actions as citizen and teacher, he was guilty of impiety and corrupting the morals of the young and his defense was sophistical, for he tricked Meletus into confusing impiety to the gods of Athens with atheism and he confused the morality of conformity determined by mores with the morality of integrity determined by the good, yet his punishment rightly should be a reward for opening to his fellow citizens a vision of piety and morality. Moreover, if justice for each man consists in performing his proper function, Socrates was just, and he should conform to the decision of law, when common opinion would have thought him justified to escape given the opportunity, since it is worse to do than to suffer injustice. This was a morality which found its basis both in force of custom and in transvaluation of values, without yielding either to the fears of innovation of the common man or the pretensions to uniqueness of the superman.

The continuation of the paradoxes of Socrates has been a debate over *which* of the contradictory propositions in each pair is in fact true, much as his trial seems to have turned on an issue that could not be stated openly because the amnesties promulgated at the end of the war prevented raising the question, was Socrates responsible for Alcibiades and Critias? Were his philosophic inquiries inconsistent with the virtues of democracy? The ironies of history, scholarship, and philosophic controversy—which were explored with irresponsible irony in examining and inventing Socratic paradoxes above—arise from simple and dogmatic efforts to affirm *one* of the contradictory propositions implied in his paradoxes, while their hidden strength and continuity derive from the unexamined recognition that more is involved in his questions and his attitude than either of the opposed positions. The issue he posed was not a choice between the truth and the recognition that any proposition is in a sense true and defensible. It was a recognition that accepted opinions and demonstrated doctrines can be saved from rigidity, and therefore from falsity and injustice, by recognizing their common inadequacies, and they can be lifted to a higher level of truth and practical efficacy by recognizing the common truth they state partially. The Socratic irony joins the contradictions which doctrinaire historical, social, and philosophic ironies separate, and it makes the tragedy of decision in confused circumstances a recognition of values which can be an inspiration, as the career of Socrates has been, rather than a defeat or an error to be lamented or deprecated.

The basic problem of the choice of Socrates is unaffected by the paradoxes of history, policy, or metaphysics. It provides, on the contrary, a guide by which the paradoxes of what men will say are resolved in the paradoxes of how man shall act. The basic problem, when one asks, "What shall a man do?" is the problem, "What is right?" or—since "right" and "just" are alternative translations of *dikaion* although their affinity is somewhat obscured in English— "What is just?" That problem is stated in two questions: "How do I know?" (and it is therefore involved in a conflict of opinions) and "Right for whom?" (and it is therefore involved in a conflict of interests). Throughout his life, Socrates argued that the guide to what a man should do is what is right, and that what is right transcends conflicts of interest (since what is good for man as man is good for all men), as well as conflicts of opinions (since differences of opinion may be removed by inquiry and virtue is knowledge). His choice is the logical outcome of this career of moral inquiry. His argument against Crito is based on the grounds of what is right—if it is not right to break the law, it is not in the interest of my family, my friends, my country, or myself, and what men say or think is irrelevant except as it bears on the right. It is not right to break the laws, as embodied in the decision of a jury, even if the decision is contrary to what one may have argued is right. The grounds of the choice and the test of what is right have not changed from an appeal to reason to an appeal to law and convention—the reason to which we appeal is an imperfect instrument which is misused, if we suppose that we have achieved an absolute truth in our inquiry or that our reason ever advances far beyond the recognition of our own ignorance, and the laws by which we are governed are imperfect guides, which we misuse if we suppose that we are justified in flouting them or distorting them to follow our own interests.

The wisdom of Socrates consists in his recognition of two sides of a single question. We destroy his insight and wisdom when we separate these two aspects, whether in criticism of Socrates and his actions or in praise of what he did and acceptance of a philosophy by which to justify it. The search for justice is a search for moral law and values above men and their societies; it is also an examination of the agreements and conventions by which men live together and engage in the search for values. Plato illustrates these two aspects of human society when he talks about freedom in two different but related senses. In the *Republic* he has Socrates define the true freedom as self-mastery, the rule in the individual of reason over impulses and passions and the rule in the state of wise counsel over the interests of groups; this freedom is contrasted to the unbridled freedom of license, by which every one does as he pleases following every unchecked impulse and whim.[21] The perfect state, Socrates adds, never did or will exist, but its citizens live in actual states. In the *Laws,* Plato has the Athenian Stranger distinguish between complete "freedom" unfettered by authority and the freedom which consists in voluntary slavery to elected magistrates and established laws.[22]

The appeal of Socrates to reason in the *Apology* and to law in the *Crito* express recognition that the irrationalities and disorders of unfettered freedom are rectified and held in control by reason or by elected magistrates and established law, and that law approximates reason in securing the harmony and agreement of men. Two mistakes are possible if we separate these two aspects of justice and freedom. We might suppose, on the one hand, that we had discovered, by reason or dialectic or science, the historical processes or material grounds or ideal purposes which identify some one state— the Prussia of Hegel or the Soviet Union of Lenin or, by an inverted dialectic, any state opposed to these—with the perfect state or its necessary antecedent in evolution; and from that point on, the search for justice is reduced to acceptance of unexamined dogma and the operation of law is transformed to the use of force and acquiescence in its use. Or, we might suppose that the democratic law under which

---

[21] *Republic,* iv. 430E–431D and viii. 557A–558C.
[22] *Laws,* iii. 698A–700A.

we live can be preserved from subversion only by excluding from its privileges and from the inquiry by which it is supported all those who do not believe in reason or freedom; and from that point on, we reduce inquiry to unreasoning conformism by fear and undermine our laws by introducing extraordinary procedures and unpredictable retrospective criteria by which to determine piety and loyalty.

The death of Socrates was a tragedy in which a citizen of the perfect city in which men are ruled by reason was judged, because of his reliance on reason, to be disloyal to an actual city whose achievements in thought and expression have been unexampled. His tragedy was not a defeat or a frustration, for he had no reason to fear the penalties he suffered and he did not swerve from the values he sought and celebrated. His death marked the tragedy of Greece and of philosophy; but they were tragedies of defeat and frustration—a decline of civilization and a failure of reason. Both tragedies have had lessons for men in general and for philosophers in particular in all later ages of Western civilization—inspiration from the tragedy of insight and catharsis, warning from the tragedy of dispossessed power and disregarded dogma. They have a particular lesson for our age. The advance of knowledge has given a new meaning to the Socratic formula, Knowledge is virtue. During the Renaissance his proposition was converted into Knowledge is power, and since the Renaissance we have forgotten the original meaning of virtue and its associations with power. The increase of power due to the advance of knowledge has brought us to a realization, more concrete and cogent than the conclusions of rational arguments, that we shall not have knowledge or virtue or power if we put limits on inquiry other than those imposed by consideration of what is true and what is right. We have resources for justice that have never existed before, and we have stumbled, in using them, into the beginnings of a world community based on a recognition of human dignity. We shall have no justice or peace, in the world or in our nations, unless we can relate interests with right and unless we can answer the questions put by Socrates to Crito—are we guided by the right, or by what we suppose men will think or say, by fear of loss of reputation, property, or even life? Can we continue the process by which respect for the law and obedience are increased by the discussion and criticism which diminishes injustice and extends the rule of law? Or must we risk anarchy by demanding acquiescence to privileged orthodoxies and to established parties and power? The choice of Socrates suggests that it is not a choice between interests and justice, but a choice of creating a tragic opposition of our honor, safety, and wealth to the demands of justice or of recognizing that there is no opposition unless values are reduced to interests, that interests are grounded in right and freedom, and that right and freedom are realized in discussion which is the only warrant for truth and in the rule of law which is the only warrant for justice.

XI

HAPPINESS AS THE GOAL

(Euripides: *The Bacchae*)

BY

WHITNEY J. OATES

I wonder what devil got into the fashioner of the program for this series of talks who selected as my subject the problem of happiness and its relation to Euripides's *Bacchae*. For all classicists the *Bacchae* of Euripides means a play which is absolutely, totally, and completely enigmatic, so therefore as I address myself to the relation between the problem of happiness and this play of Euripides, please give me your sympathy in advance.

The Greeks had a word for happiness. It is *eudaemonia*. And in a sense, the very word, *eudaemonia,* embodies within it the thesis which I should like to develop in this paper, namely, that you cannot talk or think about happiness without seeing it in a religious dimension, for right in the middle of the Greek word *eudaemonia* is *daemon* and you can think of *daemon* in any way you want.

Perhaps it may be desirable to begin our discussion by examining two Greek philosophic analyses of the problem of happiness, both deriving from the fourth century. Of course, I am thinking of Plato and Aristotle, who were writing two or three generations after the composition and first production of Euripides's *Bacchae*.

The first position I should like to review briefly is that of Aristotle. He, as you know, in the *Nicomachean Ethics* wrote the bible of *eudaemonism,* that is, the bible of happiness as the end of human life. By happiness, he means living well, and he defines it in these terms as "an activity of soul in accordance with virtue, and if there are more than one virtue, in accordance with the best and most complete." But we must add "in a complete life." "For one swallow does not make a summer, nor does one day, and so, too, one day, or a short time, does not make a man blessed and happy."[1]

It is notorious that in Aristotle's system it is rather hard to connect his theology, that is, his conception of the Unmoved Mover, of God as contemplation of contemplation, νόησις νοήσεως, with the phenomena and predicaments of human life, and so one might expect in the *Nicomachean Ethics* a delineation of happiness as the goal of life without the religious dimension which I regard as essential. But even in the *Nicomachean Ethics* Aristotle cannot avoid completely this notion, as is evident in the eloquent passage in the tenth book where he is describing the activity of reason which is contemplative. This activity is the highest kind of life, and it above all will bring the highest kind of happiness. Listen to Aristotle's words. "But such a life would be too high for man; for it is not in so far as he is man that he will live so, but in so far as something divine is present in him; and by so much as this is superior to our composite nature is its activity superior to that which is the exercise of the other kind of virtue. If reason is divine, then, in comparison with man, the life according to it is divine in comparison with human life. But we must not follow those who advise us, being men, to think of human things, and, being mortal, of mortal things, but must, so far as we can, make ourselves immortal, and strain every nerve to live in accordance with the best thing in us; for even if it be small in bulk, much more does it in power and worth surpass everything."[2] So even in Aristotle, where you might think that there would be no mention of the religious dimension involved in the problem of happiness, we do find it expressed specifically in this particular passage.

Now let us examine Plato's treatment of the problem. In the *Republic,* early in the second book, as you may recall, two interlocutors of Socrates, Glaucon and Adeimantus, as friendly advocates of the devil say that, though they really agree basically with Socrates about the superiority of justness over injustice and they agree basically

---

[1] *Nicomachean Ethics,* 1098a 13–19, Ross's translation.
[2] *Nicomachean Ethics,* 1177b26–1178a2.

that the possession of justice will guarantee happiness or living well, they wish to put the case for the opposition in its most extreme form. First they want to rule out any doctrine of divine rewards and punishments. And after having done so, they present this challenge: who will be the happier man, the most just man who *seems* to be the most unjust and hence suffers all the tortures of this world for his seeming injustice—to quote, ". . . he will be thrown into prison, he will be scourged and racked, he will have his eyes burned out, and after every kind of torment he will be crucified." [3] In contrast is the most completely unjust man who *seems* to be the most completely just, who because of his seeming justness received all the rewards, glories, powers, wealth, and honors of this world. Then just as if to make sure that it really makes no difference with respect to the gods and the doctrine of rewards and punishments, the devil's advocates submit the then current three heresies with respect to the gods and religion. The first is the heresy of atheism. There are no gods. Second, there are gods, but they have no concern for human affairs. Third, there are gods, and indeed they do have concern for human affairs, but they can be bought off with pleasing prayers and sacrifices. In other words, this latter is the heresy which involves *do ut des* religion, that is, religion strictly on a business basis. Hence, since on any one of these three grounds religion is rendered irrelevant, Glaucon and Adeimantus maintain that it is far better to be unjust while keeping up the appearance of justness. This is the challenge to Socrates who stoutly maintains that the first man, no matter what his sufferings, if he really possesses justice, will be the happier. And in a sense the remainder of the *Republic* records Socrates's answer to this challenge. But note, at the very end of the dialogue Plato will not conclude his analysis of justice and its relation to happiness without reintroducing his doctrine of the immortality of the soul, and his belief that the gods do mete out rewards and punishments after death.

In effect, Plato here is affirming that it is impossible to consider with any profundity at all the question of human happiness without seeing it in a religious perspective. In other words, happiness is in the

[3] *Republic,* II, 361e.

center of a religious context and so we have these perfectly marvelous words at the very end of the *Republic* where Socrates says: "If you will believe with me that the soul is immortal and able to endure all good and ill, we shall keep always to the upward way and in all things pursue justice with the help of wisdom. Then we shall be at peace with Heaven and with ourselves, both during our sojourn here and when, like victors in the games collecting gifts from their friends, we receive the prize of justice; and so, not here only, but in the journey of a thousand years of which I have told you, we shall fare well," εὖ πράττωμεν,—"we shall have achieved happiness." [4]

You may well ask, what has all this got to do with the *Bacchae*? Since everyone agrees that the play is really one of the most difficult pieces in all literature to interpret, I suggest that we look at the *Bacchae* as it presents what is involved, if one really does accept the postulate of Plato and Aristotle that one cannot think with any depth at all about the problem of human happiness except when it is seen in the context of religion. I shall try, therefore, to emphasize this aspect of the *Bacchae* by means of a running commentary on the play in which I shall attempt to resume its general structure with appropriate stress upon those parts which have to do with the theme of happiness.

The significant event prior to the opening of the play is the birth of the god Dionysus. Zeus in thorough conformity with his erotic virtuosity had at one time fallen in love with Semele, daughter of Cadmus, the king and founder of the city of Thebes. As a result of this love Semele became pregnant, but she was not satisfied, and consequently begged Zeus to appear to her in all his majesty. Zeus obliged by appearing in a flash of lightning which unfortunately consumed Semele, but Zeus saved the child, opened, as the myth tells us, his own flesh, concealed the child within it until it had reached the stage when it could be born a second time. (This curious feature of the Dionysiac myth has a mystic significance which need not concern us now.) So we have Dionysus born under these strange circumstances, really a latecomer in the Olympian canon. But he became the god of fertility and wine about whom a mystic and

[4] *Ibid.*, X. 621b.

orgiastic cult grew up, and indeed there is plenty of evidence for the existence and power of this cult well into historic times.

As the play opens, Dionysus in the guise of a Lydian stranger, a character from the Near East, returns to Thebes where the scene is laid, and it is he who speaks the prologue. With him is the troop of Asiatic devotees, the women who are the Bacchae. He tells us at once that he is going to take revenge upon this, his mother's city, for it has repudiated the religion of Dionysus. We are also told that Cadmus, the old founder, has turned his power over to his grandson, Pentheus, son of Agave, a sister of Semele. Furthermore, as a first step in working this revenge we learn that Agave and the other women of Thebes have already become mystically possessed by the god and are engaged in orgiastic rites in the neighboring forest of Mt. Cithaeron.

The chorus in its opening song gives its first expression to our theme of happiness, and we must not forget that the members of the chorus here are enthusiasts, that is to say, they are "possessed" genuinely by the god. They sing:

> Blesséd, blesséd is he;
> who knows the sacred rite,
> who hallows his life,
> who loses his life to live,
> reborn in the life of the band,
> who dances on the mountain,
> is purged and made whole—[5]

And then by a kind of a contrast the god himself is described in contradictory terms both horrifying and inspiring.

> He is sweet on the mountain
> He drops to the ground from the running packs!
> He wears the holy faun-skin.
> He hunts the goat and kills it.
> He delights in the raw flesh.
> He runs to the mountains of Phrygia, to the
> mountains of Lydia.

[5] *The Bacchae*, ll. 72–77. The translations are all taken by special permission from a new version by William Arrowsmith, as yet unpublished.

> He is Bromios who leads us. Evohé
> With milk the earth flows; it flows with wine,
> It flows with the nectar of bees.[6]

Next in the play comes a semicomic scene where the two old men, Cadmus, the former king of Thebes, and Teiresias, the traditional blind Greek seer, are revealed as also possessed by the god and on their way to join the revels. They are both portrayed as supremely happy, when they are interrupted by the entrance of the young king, Pentheus, who vows he will rid the city of this religious pest, asserting that it is a veil for sexual lusts and all other kinds of enormities. He berates the old men, but Teiresias, the seer, berates him in return, reminds him of the bounty of Dionysus, and warns him not to believe that political power in and of itself is something which dominates life. Pentheus threatens further, but the old men go off to the revels, and here the chorus sings again about the god. And again we must remember that the chorus is made up of orgiasts who are possessed of the god.

> Far in the air of heaven,
> the gods of heaven live.
> But they see the lives of men.
> And what passes for wisdom is not.
> For superhuman thoughts
> the price is death.[7]

And continuing in this elevated strain a bit later:

> He (Dionysus) hates the man who hates
> To live the blesséd life
> By day and dearer night,
> who will not wisely keep his heart
> Clear of clever men.
> Whatever simple people do,
> Whatever they believe
> I believe and do.[8]

[6] *Ibid.*, ll. 135–143.
[7] *Ibid.*, ll. 392–397.
[8] *Ibid.*, ll. 424–432.

This, of course, is a moving statement of the purity of the religion of simple folk, and no doubt it expresses part of Euripides's attitude toward the Dionysiac cult.

Next comes the potent scene where Pentheus holds Dionysus captive in his guise as a Lydian stranger. Pentheus arrogantly insults him, and then causes him to be thrown into a dungeon. But after a short chorus, lightning flashes, Dionysus's voice is heard off-stage, the palace trembles, and Dionysus appears calmly to report how he has toyed with Pentheus, infuriated, humiliated, and frustrated him. While he, the god, calmly liberated himself, Pentheus, the tyrannous king, has exhausted himself in pursuing and fighting with phantoms created by the god. As can easily be seen, at this point the whole tone of the play has been transformed. Dionysus is master of the situation and coldly goes about the business of revenge.

Here Euripides, by way of a break in the dramatic action, introduces a messenger's speech which first describes, in poetry of extraordinary beauty, the Theban Maenads, the female orgiasts, as they awake on Mt. Cithaeron. It depicts in essence what is to be found in genuine religious communion with nature. The messenger then reports that, when suddenly the women discover they were being watched, they were transformed by madness, and immediately swept with religious frenzy. They seize animals in their ecstasy, they tear them to pieces, and they smear themselves with blood. We cannot fail to note that in this one messenger's speech Euripides is again presenting the ambivalence he sees in religion.

The next scene presents Dionysus taking "possession" of Pentheus. After possessing him, he makes Pentheus agree to dress himself like a Maenad, and to go to observe the revels himself. And here the catlike cruelty of Dionysus is terrifyingly underscored. After Pentheus withdraws into the palace to attire himself, Dionysus defines more carefully the kind of punishment he has in store for Pentheus, and he ends this gruesome description by saying:

> He will come to know
> Dionysus, son of Zeus, consummate god,
> most terrible, most gentle to mankind.[9]

9 *Ibid.*, ll. 859–861.

And again the chorus takes up the theme:

> Slow but unmistakable
> the might of the god moves on.
> It punishes that man,
> infatuate of soul
> and hardened in his pride,
> who disregards the gods.
> The gods are crafty:
> they lie in wait
> a long step of time
> to hunt the unholy.[10]

And the ode closes with further reflections on our theme of happiness:

> Happy is he who has escaped a storm at sea,
>> Who has come to harbor.
> Happy is he who has come up from under
>> His troubles.
> Variously one man outraces another for
>> Wealth and power.
> Ten thousand men have ten thousand hopes;
>> Some bear fruit in happiness, but others go awry.
> But the man who finds his happiness from day to day,
>> That man I call the happiest.[11]

We should note the two points emphasized in the ode: first, that the god is cruel, crafty, and "lies in wait." And, second, that the man who finds his happiness from day to day, is the happiest. In other words, here are answers to the questions, what is God and whence happiness.

As if Euripides was not satisfied with one scene of Dionysus toying with Pentheus, he now twists the knife by presenting Pentheus grotesquely attired as a Maenad, and totally under the spell of the god. He is ironically insulted in even intenser terms, and just as this scene is almost too much for the audience to bear, Pentheus and Dionysus depart for Mt. Cithaeron. The chorus then sings in praise of the justice which the god is about to work, but not without another reference to happiness.

---

[10] *Ibid.*, ll. 882–890.
[11] *Ibid.*, ll. 902–911.

Death will mend his madness. For happiness, the gods require acceptance absolute from man. What the world calls wisdom, I do not want. Not here the hunt for happiness; I hunt the greater way, the great accepted goal. To live the blessed life, this is the way I go: to reject what is not right, to glorify the gods! [12]

And now we come to the most horrible part of the play as a messenger describes how the Maenads discovered Pentheus spying upon them from a treetop, how the Maenads, led by his mother, Agave, tore the tree down, how he pleaded with his mother not to attack him saying,

> Have pity, mother. I have done wrong,
> But do not kill *your* son for *my* wrongs,[13]

and how Agave and the Maenads tore him to pieces. The starkest scene, I think, in all of literature follows. Agave enters, covered with blood, in religious frenzy, holding her son's head impaled upon her thyrsus, the Maenad's magic wand, believing it to be a lion's head. She is in ecstasy. She says, "I struck him first, the Maenads call me 'Happy Agave.'" [14] Or a little later, "I am happy. I have done great things, things clear and great with my hunting." [15]

At this point Cadmus enters with the body of Pentheus, sees Agave in horror, and says that this is "a sight not happy." [16] but Agave, still religiously intoxicated, calls herself and Cadmus blessed because of her exploits and urges that Pentheus the son be summoned as she says, ". . . so he can see me in my happiness." [17] Nowhere, I think, can one find a better or more intense expression of Euripides's ambivalent attitude toward religion and happiness. Cadmus calls the sight, οὐκ εὐδαίμονα (not happy), while Agave calls herself εὐδαίμων, happy. There is no need to dwell here on the heartrending scene of Agave as she finally discovers that it is the head of her son which she is carrying.

[12] *Ibid.*, ll. 1002–1010.
[13] *Ibid.*, ll. 1120–1121.
[14] *Ibid.*, ll. 1179–1180.
[15] *Ibid.*, ll. 1197–1199.
[16] *Ibid.*, l. 1232.
[17] *Ibid.*, l. 1258.

So the play ends by the repentance of Cadmus and Agave as they see the suffering and the ruin that is caused by blaspheming the god. Dionysus appears and ordains further punishment for both Agave and Cadmus. And here we have this strange and provocative colloquy between Cadmus and Dionysus:

Cadmus says, "We implore you, Dionysus, we have sinned."

The god replies, "You have found too late who I am. Then when you should have known me, you did not."

Cadmus: "We have learned. But you deal too hardly with us."

Dionysus: "I am a god. I was blasphemed by you."

Cadmus: "Gods should not show the passions of men."

Dionysus: "Long ago my father Zeus ordained these things." [18]

What does it all mean? I think, or at least I should like to suggest, that in this play, we have a dramatic expression of the notion which later the two philosophers, Plato and Aristotle, formulated. Perhaps there are two general legitimate implications: first, the *Bacchae* suggests that happiness can come only from God, and in this sense happiness in the play is attributed only to those who are rightly or genuinely possessed by the god. But Euripides is also saying that if man's "possession" leads to frenzy, then the consequences are dreadful. And the other implication seems to be that God must be in a real sense just (and surely Euripides is maintaining this), but in the presentation of the extreme and unmitigated cruelty of Dionysus, Euripides, I think, is insisting implicitly by his stern critique of the excesses of the Dionysiac religion, that the real God, the God worthy of man's worship must be conceived of not only as just, but also as merciful.

[18] *Ibid.*, ll. 1344–1349.

XII

THE CHOICE OF ANTIGONE

(Sophocles: *Antigone*)

BY

JOHN F. C. RICHARDS

Twenty-four hundred years ago a play was produced in the city of Athens which has profoundly stirred the imaginations of men. This is not only because its author, Sophocles, was a great poet and a master of the art of the theater, but also because he presented in a vivid form a great moral problem, a problem which is universal in its scope and belongs not only to the fifth century before Christ but to all ages. This is the eternal conflict between man's law and God's law, between the decrees of a manmade state and the voice of man's conscience, that still small voice within each one of us which bids us do God's will and walk in justice and mercy.

If we listen to that voice, there are some things which no earthly ruler can make us do. We can still use the words of the Greek Stoic Cleanthes, who tells us we must all obey God's will in the end. "I shall follow you," he says, "without hesitation, but if I become base and refuse, nonetheless I shall follow you." [1]

But it is often hard to know at what point the State's law conflicts with the law of God. The New Testament gives us practical advice: "Render unto Caesar the things which are Caesar's and unto God the things that are God's." [2] It is obvious that we must pay our taxes, if the State is to be administered. Few today would approve of Thoreau's excessive individualism; for no one can be completely self-sufficient. Even Thoreau must have an ax, if he is to build his

[1] Preserved by Epictetus, Encheiridion 53.
[2] St. Matthew, 22, 21.

house in the wilderness. But when the State interferes with a man's sincere religious beliefs, then he must resist these encroachments on his liberty. This spirit of resistance has been a great and vital part of the American heritage. When the Pilgrim Fathers had crossed the Atlantic in search of this freedom of belief, Roger Williams even left Massachusetts for Rhode Island, because his fellow citizens would not allow him enough of it.

But in this cruel twentieth century we have seen the lengths to which totalitarian governments will go in denying to their subjects this precious freedom of conscience. In many parts of the world there is far less chance of successful resistance and the danger of disobedience is far greater than it was before the days of our modern secret police, thought-control, and "brain-washing."

When Sophocles wrote his play about Antigone, the issue was less complicated. The plot is a simple one. The two sons of Oedipus, who were the brothers of Antigone, had both fallen in battle; Eteocles was fighting for the city-state of Thebes, and Polyneices was fighting against it. Creon, the new ruler of Thebes and the uncle of Antigone, thought that Polyneices, who from his point of view was a traitor to the State, ought not to receive the rites of burial. Eteocles was buried with honor, but his brother was to be left as a prey for the birds and dogs.

When one of the guards reported that some unknown person had sprinkled dust on the dead man's body, Creon at once suspected that the men had been bribed.[3] The guard was threatened and dismissed, and it is at this point in the play that the Theban Elders, who form the chorus, sing their magnificent song about the achievements of mankind.

"Wonders are many," they say, "and none is more wonderful than man."[4] It is man who crosses the sea and plows the earth, who snares the birds and beasts, and tames the horses and the bulls. He has taught himself speech and wind-swift thought, and has learned how to escape the frost and rain. He has resource for all things; it is only from death that he will find no escape. Cunning is the skill through

[3] *Antigone*, 293–294.
[4] *Ibid.*, 332 ff.

which man comes now to evil, and now to good. When he honors the laws of the land, his city stands high; but a man who has sin for his companion has no city. In this brief paraphrase of the chorus the unknown person who has disobeyed Creon's edict is the man who is clever in the wrong way, and Creon presumably is the man who honors the laws and makes his city stand high. But before the play is over, he will experience the tragic *peripeteia,* the sudden reversal of fortune.

It was Antigone who insisted on disobeying Creon's edict, and when she was caught, he felt obliged to punish her, even though she was related to him. She knew that the penalty was death and she was willing to accept it.

But there was no question of torture; no one tried to tamper with her mind or distort her personality. This is the diabolical contribution of our modern totalitarian governments. Here the word "diabolical" is used deliberately; for this kind of cruelty, this attempt to warp the soul is surely a true mark of what we mean by the Devil. Our ancestors were far more conscious than we are of the actual presence of the Devil, but recently we have seen how devilish men can become, when they lose their respect for the precious quality of each man's soul and its importance to God. We can now see more clearly why it was fatal for Faust to sell his soul to the Devil.

George Orwell has shown us in his horribly prophetic book, *1984,* what is the ultimate degradation for man; after his hero had been changed by diabolical methods into something other than himself, he ended by actually loving the ruler known as "Big Brother."

Antigone, then, was willing to risk death for the sake of her principles. Creon's denial of the rites of burial was profoundly shocking to an ancient Greek. If a body was left unburied, this was an affront to the gods. When Odysseus visited the world of the dead in Homer's *Odyssey,* Elpehor, who had been left unburied at his death, met him and said: "Do not leave me unwept and unburied as you go from here nor turn your back upon me, lest I bring the wrath of the Gods upon you." [5] And Palinurus, the helmsman in Virgil's *Aeneid* who fell into the sea, made the same appeal to

[5] *Odyssey,* ll. 72–73.

Aeneas, when he visited the Lower World: [6] There Aeneas saw the souls of the dead by the river's bank, who "stood begging to be the first to be carried across and stretched forth their hands in their longing for the farther shore"; [7] but some of them were left behind by the ferryman because they were unburied.

Here Virgil expresses for a Roman audience a belief which must have been very real to a Greek like Antigone. How could she leave her brother unburied? It would be a wicked thing to do, even though he was regarded as a traitor by the government. She did not hesitate for a moment; she defied her rulers, she deceived the guards, and she sprinkled dust upon his body in simple burial service of her own.

To us she seems a heroic figure, but there was a great deal to be said on both sides of the question, as is true in all great dilemmas. Creon was foolish in giving such an order; he ought not to have interfered in what was really a religious and not a political question. And when he found that he was opposed by his own son, Haemon, and by the seer Teiresias, he ought not to have attributed base motives to them and refused to listen to their arguments. Haemon was dismissed as being a woman's champion, [8] and Teiresias was actually accused of acting "for the sake of gain." [9] According to Creon, "the whole race of prophets loves money." [10] His fault was the sin of stubborn self-will, but he was not a bad man. The heroes who suffer in Greek tragedy are not bad men, with whom the audience would feel no sympathy; they are usually good men like Oedipus, Antigone's father, who have some flaw in their character which drives them slowly to their fall.

Creon was so indignant with Polyneices because of his treachery to the State that Creon could not bring himself to be just to him, even after his death. Creon gave the order and then felt he could not alter it. Antigone disobeyed the order, but if she were to be excused, the laws would be undermined. In Creon's view, "there is no evil greater

---

[6] *Aeneid*, 6, 365 ff.
[7] *Ibid.*, 6, 313-314.
[8] *Antigone*, 740.
[9] *Ibid.*, 1047.
[10] *Ibid.*, 1055.

than lawlessness," and here he uses the Greek word from which "anarchy" is derived. "It is this," he says, "that ruins cities." [11]

There is no question that Antigone broke the law. It is even possible to argue that it was her duty to obey Creon's edict and meanwhile to work by every means for its repeal. But that would not have been in keeping with her character. The Greeks would have thought her a difficult person. And her fault was increased by the mere fact that she was a woman asserting herself in public at a time when a woman's place was in the home.

Pericles himself expresses this view in the Funeral Speech reported by Thucydides, when he says: "Great is the glory of a woman . . . when there is least talk about her among men, either for praise or blame." [12] Early feminists like Medea, a gifted woman who was not given full scope in a man's world, were sure to come to a bad end. So what must men have thought about Antigone, who was interfering with their cherished privileges? Her sister, Ismene, a gentle soul who was horrified at the idea of disobeying Creon's edict, was much more to their taste. She is the perfect foil to Antigone, timid where her sister is bold but nonetheless devoted to her. But Antigone is less than fair to her, for when Ismene finally offers her help, she rejects it and insists on acting on her own. [13]

There can be no question that her motive in disobeying Creon was a noble one; she felt that God's law was so much more important than man's law that she was willing to lay down her life in its defense. In a magnificent passage she tells Creon that it was not Zeus who published the edict. "I did not think," she says, "that your edicts had such power that one who is mortal could prevail over the sure, unwritten statutes of the Gods. For they do not live for today and yesterday, but for ever, and no one knows when they first appeared." [14] There are few passages in Greek literature that are more inspiring than this. And Sophocles expresses the same idea in a chorus of the *Oedipus Tyrannus*, where he speaks of "those laws sublime, which

[11] *Ibid.*, 672–673.
[12] Thucydides, 2, 45.
[13] *Antigone*, 538 ff.
[14] *Ibid.*, 453–457.

came to life throughout the highest heaven, whose father is Olympus alone." [15]

Antigone proclaims her belief in these unwritten and eternal laws of God, and she deserves the highest praise for setting this splendid example. It is the divine will that all men should receive the rites of burial. There can be no exceptions to this rule. And this leads to the great problem of the play and one of the most difficult textual questions in Greek literature. After the first excitement has worn off and Antigone begins to reflect on the death that awaits her, it is only natural that she should show some human weakness, and she cries out to the chorus: "Unwept and friendless, with no marriage-song, I am led out in sorrow on this journey that awaits me." [16] But instead of holding fast to her principles she begins to weaken them by implying that there are exceptions to the rule. She has disobeyed Creon's edict for the sake of a brother, but if she had been a mother and had lost one of her children, or if she had lost her husband, she might not have acted in this way. For she might have had another child or she might have married another husband, but since her mother and father were both dead, she could never have another brother.[17]

It is almost certain that these lines are an interpolation and were not in the original play as written by Sophocles. They limit the validity of the divine law and spoil the effect of Antigone's action.

They may have been added by Iophon, the son of Sophocles, or by another poet of inferior powers, or they may have been inserted by the actors, who frequently made additions to the plays. Four of the lines [18] are regarded by Sir Richard Jebb as unworthy of Sophocles, and in his Cambridge text of the play he brackets seventeen lines [19] as probably spurious.

One cause of confusion is that Aristotle quotes two of these lines [20] in his work on *Rhetoric* [21] and must have had this passage in his text

---

[15] *Oedipus Tyrannus*, 865–868.

[16] *Antigone*, 876–878.

[17] *Ibid.*, 905–912.

[18] *Antigone*, 909–912.

[19] *Ibid.*, 904–920.

[20] *Ibid.*, 911–912.

[21] *Rhetoric*, 3, 9, 16.

of the play. But it may have been interpolated before he wrote his *Rhetoric*. If this was written after his return to Athens in 335 B. C., it was over a hundred years after the play was written. The date of the *Antigone* is about 441 B. C., for the Argument at the beginning of the play states that because of the success of the *Antigone* Sophocles was appointed a general for the expedition against Samos. This took place in 440 B. C.

It is possible that the lines were added as an echo of a popular story in the history of Herodotus,[22] which expresses the same idea. When King Darius promised the wife of Intaphernes to spare the life of one of her kinsmen who were in prison, she chose to save her brother rather than her husband or one of her children, because she could never have another brother. This emphasis on the tie binding a sister to a brother is in keeping with the Greek thought of the fifth century B. C., but it does not seem appropriate in the setting of this play, where Antigone has been proclaiming a universal principle. In fact, Goethe in his conversations with Eckermann, hoped that scholars would prove the passage to be spurious, since Antigone here advances a motive which seems to him *"ganz schlecht."* [23]

There is no need to list the arguments of the scholars who have written on both sides of this question, but it may perhaps be assumed that Sophocles himself did not weaken Antigone's stand in this way. Antigone, then, was prepared to die for a principle which applies to all men. Creon ordered her to be sealed up in a cave, so that he would not actually be guilty of shedding the blood of his own niece, but eventually she would be bound to die in such a prison. Finally, after he had refused to listen to Teiresias, the Theban Elders of the chorus persuaded him to change his mind. But with characteristic rigidity he thought first of the dead and then of the living, and so his repentance came too late. First he buried the body of Polyneices, and then he went to the cave to release Antigone. His son, Haemon, had already broken into the cave and there Antigone had hanged herself; Haemon drove his father out and then killed himself at the side of the woman he loved.

But Creon's punishment was not complete; on hearing the news

[22] Herodotus, 3, 119.
[23] Eckermann, *Gespraeche mit Goethe*, 582.

of her son's death his wife, Eurydice, also killed herself. It is the tragedy of human life that so often we gain wisdom too late. In the *Agamemnon* Aeschylus teaches the lesson that "wisdom comes through suffering" [24] and at the end of the *Antigone* Sophocles says that "wisdom is the most important part of happiness, and there must be no irreverence toward the Gods." [25]

Creon at last learned wisdom but at a terrible price. He was unwise to make a law which conflicted with religion and with the conscience of his people. He was right in thinking that laws must be obeyed, if the State is to be governed well. He was wrong in refusing to listen to advice, when he was asked to repeal a bad edict.

Antigone was unwise in disobeying the law until all possible steps had been taken by the Elders to bring about its repeal, but she was noble in her willingness to face death for the sake of what she regarded as God's higher law.

Today our modern tyrants are not likely to be interested in questions of burial. Antigone's problem is not our problem, but other dangers, which are far greater, now await us. "Insolence breeds the tyrant," [26] says Sophocles; "power tends to corrupt and absolute power corrupts absolutely," says Lord Acton. And when governments are dominated by a spirit of evil, they commit terrible sins.

It is a sin to corrupt little children and make them betray their parents to the secret police.

It is a greater sin to alter a man's mind and warp his personality.

It is a most monstrous sin to destroy other men, who are all brothers in the sight of God, because of race, color, or creed.

We need a thousand leaders like Antigone in every community to keep the fires of conscience burning brightly, but they must not be hasty and reckless in their actions. They need wisdom to know what action is possible at any given time. But if they do have to face the test that Antigone faced with such courage, they can go to their death in the calm spirit of the great Roman Stoic, Thrasea Paetus, whose end is described in the last surviving chapter of the *Annals* of

[24] *Agamemnon*, 177.
[25] *Antigone*, 1347-1352.
[26] *Oedipus Tyrannus*, 873.

Tacitus. A young quaestor had come to announce the Senate's decision, and as Thrasea cut the arteries in his arms, he said to him: "We pour out a libation to Jupiter the Deliverer. Look, young man, and may the Gods avert the omen, but you have been born into times in which it is well to fortify the spirit with examples of courage." [27]

[27] *Annals,* 16, 35.

XIII

THE CONFLICT OF TRADITION AND EXPERIENCE

(The Book of Job)

BY

ROBERT GORDIS

I

Ever since Matthew Arnold called attention to Hellas and Israel as the two sources of Western civilization, it has been a widespread practice to draw contrasts, eloquent or epigrammatic, between these two creative cultures. Greece was the home of philosophy and science; Palestine, of religion and morality. Hellas invented science, Israel discovered conscience. The Greek ethos was predominantly intellectual and skeptical, its highest symbol being the philosopher; the Hebrew ethos basically emotional and moral, rooted in faith, its noblest exemplar being the prophet.

The fundamental unity of the human spirit should have made us wary in advance of drawing such sharp distinctions between two peoples. As modern scholarship has explored all the facets of life in both centers, it has documented the similarities of the Greeks and the Hebrews, as well as their differences. Notable progress has been registered in the study of Greek religion, as expressed both in public rites, which spoke for the group, and in the mystery cults, which appealed to the individual. These investigations have served to reveal the emotional, nonrational aspects of the Greek spirit. Conversely, contemporary research into biblical Wisdom literature has indicated a strong intellectual cast in Jewish religious thought. Divergences undoubtedly exist between the Greek and the Hebrew spirit, but they are largely differences in emphasis, significant, to be sure, but not mutually exclusive.

Consider, for example, what may perhaps be described as the supreme embodiment of the creative genius of the two peoples, the *Dialogues of Plato* and the *Book of Job*. Here the distinctions between the two cultures are most striking. The Dialogues are, of course, the expression of an incisive intelligence, seeking to establish the proper norms of human conduct through the exercise of reason. In Books I and II of *The Republic* the effort is made to analyze the concept of justice, discarding false notions and arriving at a true understanding. It is the same theme that preoccupies the author of Job, but what a world of difference in temperament and method, in the mode of expression, and in the conclusions reached! Nowhere in Job is there analysis of the nature of right and wrong. What the Greek philosopher sought to discover through the mind, the Hebrew poet knew through the heart. It is not merely Job's antagonists in the debate who do not doubt that right is right and wrong is wrong. He himself never differs with them on the nature of righteousness. To raise such questions is possible only for sinners who wish to confuse their fellows so that they may despoil them.

> Woe unto them that call evil good,
> And good evil;
> That change darkness into light,
> And light into darkness;
> That change bitter into sweet,
> And sweet into bitter!
>
> (Isaiah 5:20) [1]

For honorable men, however, the truth was clear: "It hath been told thee, O man, what is good and what the Lord thy God doth require of thee, to do justice, to love mercy, and to walk humbly with thy God" (Micah 6:8). Man knows the good because God has revealed it to him—and justice and mercy are recognizable by their presence or absence in human affairs.

The difference, farreaching between Plato and Job, in content and temper, is reflected in striking variation of form. The Greek Dialogues are prose, the Hebrew Dialogues exalted poetry. If we seek a parallel

---

[1] The biblical passages throughout this chapter are based on translations by the author.

to Job in the Hellenic world, we must turn to Aeschylus, perhaps the most "Hebraic" of the Greeks.

Having noted the vast distinctions between Plato and Job, we should not ignore the affinities, recognizing that what is primary in the one is likely to be secondary in the other. It would be a grave error to underestimate the emotional drive underlying the ostensibly cool analysis of the Socratic dialogues. It was the poet in Plato that led him to banish poets from his Republic, for he knew the strength of the irrational, creative aspects of human nature, which brook no discipline and confound the neatest blueprints of the future. The entire structure of Platonic Ideas is a creation of the poetic faculty, a myth which seeks to interpret the nature of reality. To ignore the emotional underpinning of the Platonic dialogues is fatal to their understanding.

II

Equally disastrous is the failure to recognize the strong intellectual content of the Book of Job. It is not merely that the author of Job is, in Pfeiffer's words, the most learned ancient before Plato; indeed, he possesses a range of knowledge and perhaps of experience that recalls that of Shakespeare. The temptation of Job, the heart of the tragedy and the triumph, is, to be sure, expressed in passionately emotional terms, but it is intellectual as much as it is moral. Beyond the specific issue of the problem of suffering with which it is concerned, the book posits a problem as enduring as man himself, who remembers the past but lives in the present, and it points the way to an answer. This perennial issue is the conflict between the accepted tradition of the group and the personal experience of the individual. Though Job has suffered the full gamut of human misery, the accepted religious doctrine of his day has a ready answer: suffering is the result and consequently, the sign of sin. Heretofore, Job has never had cause to doubt the proposition, for it was a logical consequence of his faith in a world ruled by a just God. In fact, Job's prosperity and well-being was the best evidence of the truth of the conventional doctrine! Now he has been exposed to a rapid succession of calamities that have destroyed his wealth, decimated his family, and wracked his body with loathsome disease.

For his friends, the severity of Job's affliction serves only to demonstrate the gravity of his offenses. A few months before, Job himself would not have doubted the conclusion. Had it been reported to him during the period of his well-being that some individual had been visited by such devastating blows, the God-fearing Job would have reacted exactly as do his friends.

Hence the discussion does not begin as a debate at the outset. When the friends come to comfort Job in his affliction, they naturally take it for granted that his faith in unshaken. For even his tragic lament on the day of his birth (chapter 3) is couched in general terms; it is not yet directed against God. Eliphaz is certain that all that is required is to remind Job of the basic religious truth that has been momentarily darkened for him by his suffering:

> If one venture a word unto thee, wilt thou be weary? . . .
> But now it is come unto thee, and thou canst not bear it,
> It toucheth thee, and thou are affrighted. . . .
> Remember, I pray thee, who ever perished, being innocent?
>
> (Job 4:2, 5, 7)

Soon enough, Eliphaz and his colleagues discover that it is a vastly changed Job that confronts them. Job has undergone a shattering personal experience, but he knows, with the knowledge that defies all logic, that he is innocent. He must now choose between tradition and experience, between the body of convictions and beliefs accumulated by the generations, on the one hand, and the testimony of his own senses and reactions, on the other. For the individual to set himself against the generality of mankind is both a tragic and a heroic enterprise. Its pathos in Job's case is heightened by the feeling, which he himself had always shared, that the body of religious truth which he now opposes is the very bedrock of morality. His adversaries can therefore accuse him in all sincerity of undermining the foundations of society. In Bildad's words:

> Thou that tearest thyself in thine anger
> Shall the earth be forsaken for thee?

Or shall the rock be removed out of its place?
(Job 18:4)

The personal suffering involved is intense for all concerned, for Job, who now recognizes his loneliness in a world where once he was at home, and for his friends, who stand helplessly by as the chasm opens between them.

III

Job's tragedy, however, goes deeper, for he is compelled to challenge no superficial body of ideas, but the very heart and essence of biblical thought. The axis on which all of Hebrew religion turns is the tension between two poles, that of faith in God, the just Ruler of the universe, and that of the widespread phenomenon of human suffering. The profoundest spirits in Israel had labored to solve the tragic paradox of evil in God's world. In the process, an imposing body of thought had developed in which the lawgiver, the prophet, the historian, and the sage had each played a part, either in emphasizing one pole or the other, or in seeking to reconcile the contradiction throughout a theodicy justifying the ways of God to man.

At the very beginning of Israel's meeting with God, the process had begun, for the Decalogue proclaimed on Sinai rests on faith in the justice of God as an effective force in the universe. In that immortal Code, God has introduced Himself, as Judah Halevi had noted in another connection, not as the Creator of heaven and earth, but as the Author of liberty, Who had brought Israel out of the house of bondage. The implication of the First Commandment, probably not immediately apparent to all of Moses's contemporaries, was that God held universal sway and was no merely national deity, limited to his own territorial domain, like the gods of the Canaanites, the Ammonites, or the Moabites. The God of Israel, Who had delivered the weak from slavery in a foreign land and had executed judgment upon their oppressors, was by that token both all-powerful and all-just.

From this basic conviction, the Pentateuchal doctrine of retribution followed naturally—righteousness would be rewarded and wickedness would receive its condign punishment. The doctrine was expressed in the famous Deuteronomic passage:

And it shall come to pass, if ye shall hearken diligently unto My commandments which I command you this day, to love the Lord your God, and to serve Him with all your heart and with all your soul, that I will give the rain of your land in its season . . . Take heed to yourselves, lest your heart be deceived, and ye turn aside, and serve other gods, and worship them; and the anger of the Lord be kindled against you, and He shut up the heaven, so that there shall be no rain, and the ground shall not yield her fruit; and he perish quickly from off the good land which the Lord giveth you (Deuteronomy 11:13, 14, 16, 17).

The principle was elaborated with graphic power in the Comminations, which set forth the rewards of righteousness and the penalty of sin for the nation (Leviticus, chapter 26, and Deuteronomy, chapter 28).

The doctrine of retribution could be held with total conviction, because it arose early in Hebrew history, when group-consciousness was all powerful and the individual was conceived of as little more than a cell in the larger organism, whose personal destiny had no existence apart from the clan and the nation to which he belonged.

The biblical historians, the authors of Joshua, Judges, Samuel, and Kings, made the doctrine of national retribution the cornerstone of their philosophy of history, explaining the ebb and flow of Hebrew prosperity and disaster in terms of the people's fluctuating obedience or resistance to the word of God:

And they forsook the Lord, the God of their fathers, who brought them out of the land of Egypt, and followed other gods, of the gods of the peoples that were round about them, and worshipped them; and they provoked the Lord. . . . And the anger of the Lord was kindled against Israel, and he delivered them into the hands of spoilers that spoiled them, and He gave them over into the hands of their enemies round about, so that they could not any longer stand before their enemies (Judges 2: 12, 14).

The Prophet Hosea emphasized that the law of consequence was rooted in the universe, by expressing it in a metaphor drawn from nature:

For they sow the wind, and they shall reap the whirlwind; . . .
Sow to yourselves in righteousness, reap in mercy,
Break up the fallow ground,
For it is time to seek the Lord,
Till He come and teach you righteousness.
Ye have plowed wickedness, you have reaped iniquity,
Ye have eaten the fruit of lies—

(Hosea 8:7; 10:12, 13).

Hosea's older contemporary, Amos, had applied the same principle of justice as the law of history to contemporary world affairs, and found in it the key to the destiny of all the neighboring nations and not only of Israel (Amos, chapter 1, 2).

Even in its collective form, the doctrine of retribution created immense difficulties. In their effort to resolve these problems, the Prophets deepened the content of Hebrew religion. If God is all-righteous, it follows that a sinful people, even if it be Israel, deserves to perish. The Prophets of Israel loved God, but they loved their people, too, and could not make their peace with this logical but devastating conclusion. Thus Amos, confronted by the iniquitous Kingdom of Israel, which refused even to hear his message, let alone reorder its national existence, foretold the annihilation of the northern state. But the total disappearance of his people was an intolerable prospect for the Hebrew Prophet, both because of his natural attachment to his kinsmen and his conviction that God's word needed a spokesman in an idolatrous world. After his expulsion from the Northern Kingdom Amos transferred his hopes for the future to the smaller and weaker Kingdom of Judah (Amos 9:8 ff.).[2]

A generation later, his spiritual descendant, Isaiah of Jerusalem, faced the same heartrending challenge of a righteous God judging His sinful people. Incomparably the greatest intellect among the Prophets, Isaiah refined still further Amos's faith that part of the Hebrew people would survive, by enunciating his doctrine of the Saving

[2] On the transformation of Amos's thought occasioned by his expulsion from Beth-El by the priest Amaziah, see my "The Composition and Structure of Amos," *Harvard Theological Review*, vol. 33, 1940, pp. 239–251, and *cf.* W. S. McCullough, "Some Suggestions About Amos," *Journal of Biblical Literature*, vol. 72, 1953, pp. 247 ff.

Remnant. Not all of Judah, but some of Judah, would be saved. History was a process of the survival of the spiritually fittest, directed by God Who would reveal those capable of regeneration and salvation.

Another challenge confronted Isaiah's faith in the God of hosts, Who is exalted in righteousness. The Assyrian conqueror, infinitely more arrogant and cruel than Israel had ever been, was treading all other nations, including Israel, under foot. How could that spectacle of evil triumphant be reconciled with a just and almighty God? This contradiction Isaiah resolved by another profound insight, the concept of "the rod of God's anger." Assyria, pitiful in its conceit, was merely an instrument in God's hand for rooting out the evil and ushering in the good. When its function would be accomplished, it would pay the penalty for its crime against God and man!

> O Asshur, the rod of Mine anger,
> He is a staff for Mine indignation! [3]
> I send him against an ungodly nation,
> And against the people of My wrath do I command him.
> And it shall come to pass,
> That when the Lord has completed His whole work
> On Mt. Zion and on Jerusalem,
> I will punish the fruit of the king of Assyria's arrogance,
> And the glory of his haughty looks.

> For he has said:
> "By the strength of my hand I have done it,
> And by my wisdom, for I was clever,
> In that I have removed the boundaries of nations,
> And have robbed their treasures.
> And have brought down, as a mighty one, the inhabitants."

> Should the axe boast against him that wields it?
> Should the saw magnify itself against him that moveth it?

---

[3] In *b yadam*, the *mem* is the enclitic, familiar from Ugaritic, as is clear from the parallelism, and *b yad* is a phonetic variant of *b ad*, amply attested in Northwest Semitic. Hence the word is to be translated, not "in their hand" but "for." See *inter alia* my "A Note on Yad," *Journal of Biblical Literature*, vol. 62, 1943, pp. 341 ff.

> As if a rod could move him that lifts it,
> Or as if a staff could lift him that is not wood!
>
> (Isaiah 10:5, 6, 7, 12, 13, 15)

The same challenge in a far more agonizing form confronted Isaiah's anonymous namesake, Deutero-Isaiah, a century and a half later. The people of Judah were now in ignominious exile under the heel of the Babylonian empire. How explain the misery and degradation of Israel? It could not be justified in terms of Israel's sin, for, at its worst, Israel was better than its pagan conqueror. Unless these tormenting doubts were met, the people would be plunged into a despair that would be the prelude to dissolution. A message of hope and courage was needed, not only for Israel's sake, but for God's cause, for this people, weak and imperfect, remained "God's witnesses" (Isaiah 43:10). A rabbinic comment spells out the implications of the Deutero-Isaianic metaphor: "Ye are My witnesses, saith the Lord. If ye are My witnesses, I am the Lord, but if ye are not My witnesses, I am not the Lord." [4] The great Prophet of the Exile accordingly evolved the doctrine of the Suffering Servant of the Lord.[5] Israel is not merely God's witness, but man's teacher, whose suffering at the hands of the nations is evidence of their moral immaturity. These tribulations are destined to end when the nations recognize Israel's true greatness:

> Behold My servant, whom I uphold;
> Mine elect, in whom My soul delighteth;
> I have put My spirit upon him,
> He shall make the right to go forth to the nations.
> He shall not cry, nor lift up,
> Nor cause his voice to be heard in the street.
> A bruised reed shall he not break,

[4] Cited in the name of the Tannaitic sage Simeon bar Yohai in *Sifre, Deut.* sec. 346; *cf.* also *Pesikta*, ed. Buber, p. 102b and *Yalkut Shimeoni, Isaiah*, sec. 455.

[5] *Cf.* the careful study of the theme in C. R. North, *The Suffering Servant in Deutero-Isaiah*, Oxford, 1948, and the briefer survey of the various theories in H. H. Rowley, *The Servant of the Lord and other Essays*, London, 1952. The view adopted in the text, that the Servant is Israel in its ideal sense, is still the most acceptable position, particularly when the fruitful concept of "fluid personality" is taken into account. See H. W. Robinson, *The Cross of the Servant—A Study in Deutero-Isaiah*, London, 1928, and see my remarks in "Hosea's Marriage and Message," *Hebrew Union College Annual*, vol. 25, 1954, pp. 15 ff.

And the dimly burning wick shall he not quench;
He shall make the right to go forth according to the truth. . . .

Behold, My servant shall prosper,
He shall be exalted and lifted up, and shall be very high. . . .

Surely our diseases he did bear, and our pains he carried;
Whereas we did esteem him stricken,
Smitten of God, and afflicted.
But he was wounded because of our transgressions,
He was crushed because of our iniquities:
The chastisement of our welfare was upon him,
And with his stripes we were healed.

Therefore will I divide him a portion among the great,
And he shall divide the spoil with the mighty;
Because he bared his soul unto death,
And was numbered with the transgressors;
Yet he bore the sin of many,
And made intercession for the transgressors
(Isaiah 42:1-3; 52:13; 53:4, 5, 12).

Thus for the first time the Prophet affirmed the possibility of national suffering that was not the consequence of sin, but, on the contrary, an integral element in the process of the moral education of the race. This insight of Deutero-Isaiah was not lost on the author of Job.

The tension between God's justice and the triumph of wickedness was also met in another way by the Prophets, who deepened an older folkbelief in the Day of the Lord. The people had long believed that the day would come when the Lord of Israel would give His people victory over its foes and establish its hegemony over all. This chauvinistic doctrine has its parallels in ancient and in modern times among all peoples. The Hebrew Prophets did not attack or denounce the doctrine—they moralized it. They agreed that the day would come when the Lord of Israel would arise and bring victory to His cause, but that did not mean Israel, only a *righteous* Israel. For several of the Prophets, notably, Isaiah and Micah, the instrument for God's purpose in the world would be the Messiah, the anointed scion of the house of David. The Messiah would restore the scales of justice to their true balance, by ushering in freedom and plenty for Israel and peace and brotherhood for the world. The Messianic age represents the triumph of the righteousness of God in an imperfect world. Justice would prevail—what was needed was patience in the present and faith in the future.

In sum, the contradiction between the doctrine of retribution and the spectacle of injustice in the world created most of the deepest insights of biblical religion.

IV

To wait patiently for the triumph of God's retribution was relatively easy, so long as the nation was the unit under consideration, for God has eternity at His command, and nations are longlived. This is particularly the case of Israel. In Ben Sira's words:

> The life of man is but a few days,
> But the life of Jeshurun, days without number
> (Ben Sira 37:25).

Yet from the beginning the individual played a part in the religious consciousness. His hopes and desires, his fears and frustrations, could not be submerged wholly in the destiny of the nation. The people might prosper and a man might be miserable; the status of society might be critical, yet the individual could find life tolerable. The Law of God demanded obedience from the individual; was it unfair to expect that righteousness or sinfulness would receive their reward or punishment in the life of the individual as well? Imperceptibly, the problem emerged in the days of the First Temple. Isaiah had taken the simplest course by reaffirming the traditional doctrine and applying it to the individual:

> Say ye of the righteous, that it shall be well with him;
> For they shall eat the fruit of their doings.
> Woe unto the wicked! It shall be ill with him;
> For the work of his hands shall be done to him
> (Isaiah 3:10, 11).

As inexorable doom began descending on the nation and the small Judean state saw its lifeblood ebbing away, the mere reiteration of conventional ideas was not enough. Now there was no comfort or compensation in collective retribution. Moreover, since the individual was now the unit and the scale of judgment, the counsel of long range patience was pathetically irrelevant, for man flowers but a brief instant. The Prophets Jeremiah and Ezekiel, whose tragic destiny was to foretell and to witness the destruction of the Temple and the Babylonion exile, agonized over the prosperity of the wicked and the suffering of the righteous:

> Right wouldst Thou be, O Lord,
> Were I to contend with Thee,
> Yet will I reason with Thee:
> Wherefore doth the way of the wicked prosper?
> Wherefore are all the traitors secure?
>
> (Jeremiah 12:1)

Both Prophets protested energetically against the popular doctrine enshrined in a folksaying:

> The fathers have eaten sour grapes,
> And the children's teeth are set on edge
> (Jeremiah 31:28; Ezekiel 18:2).

Ezekiel in particular emphasized the doctrine of individual responsibility and individual retribution. He was content to bolster ethical living without formulating a complete theodicy. Other men of faith, psalmists and poets, urged obedience to God's will, buttressed by the faith that righteousness would soon triumph in the life of the individual:

> For His anger is but for a moment,
> His favour is for a life-time;
> Weeping may tarry for the night,
> But joy cometh in the morning
>
> (Psalms 30:6).

> The Lord is good unto them that wait for Him,
> To the soul that seeketh Him.

It is good that a man should quietly wait
For the salvation of the Lord
(Lamentations 3:25, 26).

Thus biblical religion, resting on the cornerstone of faith in a just and powerful God, met all challenges and held fast to its faith that justice prevails in God's world. Every generation in Israel had been nurtured upon this faith, drawing from it the motive for obedience to God's law, the strength to bear affliction, and the patience to await the hour of vindication.

V

Job, too, had always accepted this body of religious teaching as the truth. Then came the crisis, catastrophe following catastrophe, leaving the temple of his existence a mass of rubble. We know that Job's misery and degradation is a part of a cosmic experiment to discover whether man is capable of serving the ideal for its own sake, without the hope of reward. But Job has no such inkling—for him, *the accepted religious convictions of a lifetime are now contradicted by his personal experience,* by his unshakable knowledge that he is no sinner, certainly not sinful enough to deserve such a succession of blows upon his defenseless head.

Of Job's inner travail the friends are unaware. Eliphaz, the oldest and the wisest of the three, proceeds to remind Job of the truths by which he has lived. It is noteworthy that the author, whose sympathies are clearly on Job's side,[6] nevertheless gives the fullest and fairest presentation of the conventional theology. Divine justice does prevail in the world, the apparent contradictions in the world of reality notwithstanding. In the first instance, the process of retribution takes time and so Job must have patience. The righteous are never destroyed, while the wicked, or at least their children, are ultimately

---

[6] This is clear from the greater length and eloquence of the Job speeches and from the Divine judgment on the friends in Job 42:8. This verse is part of the "jointures" (12:11–13; 42:7–10), the links written by the poet to connect the prose tale, which he utilizes as prologue and epilogue, with the poetic dialogue. On the critical problems involved, see my study, "All Men's Book—A New Introduction to Job," *Menorah Journal,* Winter, 1947, pp. 329-358.

punished. Eliphaz then describes a vision from on high which discloses to him the truth that all men are imperfect, so that not even the righteous may justly complain if he suffers. God is not responsible for sin, for it is a human creation (vv. 6, 7). Moreover, suffering is a discipline—and hence a mark of God's love (v. 17). Ultimately, the righteous are saved and find peace and contentment.

In his later speeches, Eliphaz will emphasize the familiar doctrine of God's visiting the sins of the fathers upon the children, and will extend it, for by the side of this "vertical responsibility" linking all the generations through time, there is a "horizontal responsibility" in space, uniting all men in a given generation. Thus the entire people is visited by a plague because of King David's sin (II Samuel 24:11 ff.). On the other hand, it is this interdependence of mankind which makes it possible for the saint, by his presence, to redeem his sinful contemporaries, as when Abraham sought to save Sodom for the sake of a righteous minority. Accordingly, Eliphaz promises Job that if he repents and makes his peace with God, he will be able to intercede with Him for sinners and save them:

> Thou wilt then issue a decree, and it will be fulfilled for thee,
> And upon thy ways, light will shine.
>
> When men are brought low, thou wilt say, "Rise up!"
> And the humble will be saved.
> Even the guilty will escape punishment,
> Escaping through the cleanness of thy hands [7]
>
> (Job 22:28–30).

Job has scarcely heard, let alone been persuaded, by Eliphaz's arguments or by the considerably more heated and less illuminating speeches of the other friends. He has no theory to propose as a substitute, merely his consciousness that he is suffering without cause. He does not claim to be perfect, but insists he is not a willful sinner. Against the conventional ideas he sets the testimony of his own experience, which he will not deny, whatever the consequences. As

---

[7] *Cf.* my "Corporate Responsibility in Job," *Journal of Near Eastern Studies*, vol. 4, 1945, and the references cited there.

the round of debate continues, Job's fury mounts, as does the helpless wrath of his friends. For his attacks upon their disloyalty, his pathetic description of his physical pain and mental anguish, his indignant rejection of their deeply held faith, serve all the more to convince them that he is a sinner. For do not arrogance and the assumption of innocence by man, with the implied right and capacity to pass judgment on God, constitute the height of impiety?

Bildad paints a picture of the destruction of the wicked and the ultimate restoration of the righteous, and he hymns the power of God. Job dismisses this as irrelevant, for he does not deny God's power; it is His justice that Job calls into question. Zophar, the youngest and least discreet of the friends, summons Job to repent of his secret sins.

With bitter irony, Job turns again upon his friends who, in their security and ease, can afford to indulge in artificial arguments far removed from the painful realities of life. In a passage long misunderstood, he parodies their speeches on the greatness of God and concludes that their defense of God, dishonest and biased as it is, will not be likely to win His favor.[8]

As the first cycle ends, Job has been fortified in his conviction that he is right. What he experiences existentially cannot be refuted theoretically; it must be taken into account in any conception of reality.

Job is aware of the contention that morality depends upon faith in Divine justice. Denying the latter, how can he maintain the former? Job is driven to a desperate expedient, which is to prove one of the great liberating ideas in religion; he cuts the nexus between virtue and reward. Honest men will tremble at his undeserved suffering, but will not on that account be deterred from righteousness:

> Upright men are astonished at this,
> And the innocent stirreth up himself against the godless.
> Yet the righteous holdeth on his way,
> And he that hath clean hands waxeth stronger and stronger
> (Job 17:8, 9).

[8] For this passage *cf.* in "Quotations as a Literary Usage in Biblical, Rabbinic and Oriental Literature," *Hebrew Union College Annual,* vol. 22, 1949, pp. 214 ff.

The *Mishnah* (*Sotah* 5:5) quite correctly contends that Job served God from love and not from fear. God's ways still remain to be justified, but in the interim man's ways must be just.

In the succeeding cycles, Eliphaz adds a supplement to the traditional position.[9] He emphasizes that there is more to the punishment of the wicked than his ultimate destruction, whether in his own person or in that of his offspring. During the very period of his ostensible prosperity he lives in trepidation, never knowing when the blow will fall. Otherwise, the same ideas are reiterated, but with greater vehemence. The conventional theodicy, maintained by the friends, has exhausted itself.

VI

The full meaning of Job's existential tragedy now begins to disclose itself. Increasingly, Job has become convinced, not merely that the friends have maligned him, but that they have traduced God. In the first cycle, Job has ventured a hope that some impartial arbiter might decide between him and God:

> For He is not a man, as I am, that I should answer Him,
> That we should come together in judgment.
> Would [10] that there were an arbiter between us,
> That might lay His hand upon us both,
> Were He to take His rod away from me,
> And not let His terror make me afraid;
> I should speak, and not fear,
> For I am not so with myself.[11]

(Job 9:32-35).

As the friends proceed to attack Job's integrity with less and less restraint, the contact between Job and them all but disappears. Their conception of God is meaningless for him. He proceeds to discover

[9] The second cycle is intact, but the third cycle has suffered extensive dislocations and loss of material. For a succinct summary of attempted solutions to these problems, *cf.* R. H. Pfeiffer, *Introduction to the Old Testament*, New York, 1941, pp. 670 ff., and see the paper cited in note 5 above.

[10] Revocalizing *lo* and *lu*, with many moderns.

[11] Or, assuming a *tiqqun sopherim* or euphemistic change by the scribes (*hu* for *anokhi*) render, with Yellin, "for He is not just with me."

a new faith, forged in the crucible of his undeserved suffering, as unshakable as his experience of his own innocence—behind the cruel reality of suffering, a just order must exist in the world. He can find no sympathy or understanding among his erstwhile friends; then there must be, there would be, a witness on his behalf later:

> O earth, cover not my blood,
> And let my cry have no resting-place.
> Even now, behold, my Witness is in heaven,
> And He that testifies for me is on high.
> Are my intercessors to be my friends?
> Unto God does my eye pour out tears!
> For He would prove a man right even when he contends with God
> As between one man and his fellow!

(Job 16:18–21)

As the debate reaches a crescendo of fury, Job attains a crescendo of faith. The longing first expressed for an arbiter (*mōkhiah*) has become a conviction of a witness (*'ēdh*) ready to speak on his behalf. Now he reaches the peak of faith. In a moment of mystic ecstasy he sees his vindication through a Redeemer, Who will act to avenge his suffering. The term he uses, *gō'ēl*,[12] means a kinsman, a blood-avenger, who in earlier Hebrew law, was dutybound to see that justice was done to his aggrieved brother.

The inherent difficulties of communicating a mystic vision are aggravated by textual problems in the famous passage, which I believe should be rendered as follows:

> Oh that my words were now written!
> Oh that they were inscribed in a book!
> That with an iron pen and lead
> They were graven in the rock for ever!
> But as for me, I know that my Redeemer liveth,
> Though He be the last to arise upon earth.
> For from within my skin, this has been marked,
> And from my flesh do I see God,
> Whom I see for myself,
> My own eyes behold, not another's!

---

[12] *Cf.* Hastings, *Dictionary of the Bible,* vol. 2, pp. 222 ff., s.v. *Goel.*

But the momentary vision of God arising to redeem him fades; Job cannot hold the ecstasy—

> My veins are consumed with longing within me
> (Job 19:23–27).[13]

Similarly, the modern saint, Rabbi Abraham Isaac Kuk, has sought to describe the ecstasy of the experience of "the nearness of God" which extends beyond "the walls of deed, logic, ethics, and laws." But exaltation is followed by depression, as the mystic sinks back "into the gray and tasteless world of conflict, contradiction, and doubt." [14]

Job, however, in spite of his experience, is no mystic, who can find peace in the beatific vision. Even after the ecstasy has faded, he demands vindication. Only if God appears to him and answers, will he know that his suffering is not meaningless, that it counts for something in the universe. In his last speech, which sets forth his code of conduct, he closes with a plea:

> Oh that I had one to hear me!—
> Lo, this is my desire, that God answer me,
> And that I had the indictment my foe has written,
> I would surely carry it on my shoulder
> And bind it as a crown for myself!
> I would announce to Him the number of my steps,
> Like a prince would I confront Him!
> (Job 31:35–37)

Who is this Arbiter, this Witness, this Redeemer to Whom Job looks for salvation and comfort? Job's refuge is the God of righteousness, Who lives and rules the world behind the sway of the God of power. The dichotomy never becomes a dualism; for the Hebrew author, as for his hero, these two aspects must be one. In the end, the two aspects of the Divine emerge as one, when the God of reality not only ignores the defenses of the friends in his speeches, but

[13] On the exegesis of this crucial passage, see the exhaustive study of Julius Speer in *ZATW*, 1905, pp. 47–140, and Driver-Gray, *ICC on Job*, New York, 1921, vol. 1, pp. 170 ff.; vol. 2, pp. 126 ff.

[14] *Cf.* the brief but illuminating summary of Rabbi Kuk's religious philosophy in J. B. Agus, *Guideposts of Modern Judaism*, New York, 1954, pp. 53 f.

castigates them, "for ye have not spoken the truth about Me as has my servant Job" (42:7, 8), so that Job must intercede for them. God's power and God's righteousness, the attributes of justice and the attributes of mercy are one in Him; it is only to man's limited and imperfect gaze that they seem distinct, if not contradictory.

Centuries later, the medieval Hebrew poet, Solomon Ibn Gabirol, in his *Royal Crown,* echoed the heartbeat of Job in his affliction, but like him, retained his faith in the One Living God of the universe:

> Therefore though Thou shouldst slay me, yet I will trust in Thee.
> For if Thou shouldst pursue my iniquity,
> I will flee from Thee to Thyself,
> And I will shelter myself from Thy wrath in Thy shadow,
> And to the skirts of Thy mercies I will lay hold,
> Until Thou hast had mercy on me,
> And I will not let Thee go till Thou hast blessed me.[15]

The later poet, Immanuel of Rome rephrased the same thought:

> I shall flee for help, from Thee to Thee,
> And cover myself with Thy wings in the day of trouble,
> And from Thy wrath flee to Thy shadow.[16]

Job's final speech is no longer addressed to his friends. Like his opening lament (chapter 3), his closing confession of innocence (chapter 31) is a soliloquy.

VII

There now appears a brash young character named Elihu, of whom, we are to assume, the dignified elders have previously taken no notice. He has overheard the debate and feels impelled to inject himself into the discussion. For a variety of reasons, many scholars regard the Elihu speeches (chapters 32–39) as a later interpolation, an easy method which solves little. What has been generally overlooked is the basic fact that in the architecture of the book, Elihu's speeches

[15] *Cf.* I. Davidson, editor, *Selected Religious Poems of Solomon Ibn Gabirol,* Philadelphia, 1944, p. 118.
[16] *Cf.* his *Mahbarot,* chapter 19.

perform a vital function. Increasingly, the study of ancient literatures, like that of the Homeric epics, has been focusing attention upon the unity and meaning of the whole rather than upon the disparity of the parts. That the indiscriminate and even accidental lumping together of scattered literary fragments by an obtuse redactor, who often did not understand the material he was working with, will produce a masterpiece—that naive faith of nineteenth century literary critics is no longer widely shared today.[17]

The differences between the Elihu chapters and the rest of the book, which are fewer than is generally alleged, may perhaps be explained by the assumption that they were added by our author at a later period in his career. The creation of a masterpiece like Job might well have been a lifetime undertaking and Goethe's *Faust* is a case in point. The *Urfaust* goes back to the poet's *Sturm und Drang* period, when he was in his twenties. The first part of *Faust* did not appear until more than thirty years later, in 1808; and the second part was completed shortly before his death, more than two decades later in 1832. In the long process, Goethe's conception of his theme underwent a profound transformation. Something like that may well have been the case with the author of Job.

It is noteworthy that Elihu is at least as antagonistic to the friends as he is to Job. Actually he denies the truth of both positions. The friends have maintained that God is just and that therefore suffering

---

[17] *Cf.* the trenchant observations of H. D. F. Kitto, *The Greeks,* Harmondsworth, 1951, p. 63:

The attribution (of the *Iliad* and the *Odyssey* to Homer) was accepted quite wholeheartedly until modern times, when closer investigation showed all sorts of discrepancies of fact, style and language, both between the two epics and between the various parts of each. The immediate result of this was the minute and confident division of the two poems, but especially the *Iliad* into separate lays of different periods, appropriately called "strata" by critics, who imperfectly distinguished between artistic and geological composition. The study of the epic poetry of other races, and of the methods used by poets by working in this traditional medium, has done a great deal to restore confidence in the substantial unity of each poem; that is to say, that what we have in each case is not a short poem by one original "Homer" to which later poets have added more or less indiscriminately, but a poem, conceived as a unity by a relatively later "Homer" who worked over and incorporated much traditional material—though the present *Iliad* certainly contains some passages which were not part of Homer's original design.

is both the penalty and the proof of sin. Job has countered by insisting that his suffering is not the result of sin and therefore he charges God with injustice. Elihu denies the conclusion of both sides by injecting a virtually new idea, adumbrated in another form in Deutero-Isaiah and referred to in one verse by Eliphaz: [18] Elihu declares that God is just, and yet suffering may rightly come to the innocent, as a discipline and a warning. Job has contended that God avoids contact with man. On the contrary, Elihu insists, God does communicate with man through dreams and visions, and when these fail, through illness and suffering.

This recognition of the uses of pain is the kind of mature insight that would come to a man through years of experience: for life teaches at every hand how insufferable are those who have never suffered and that frustration and sorrow are men's passport to fellowship and sympathy with their brothers.

The author of Job would undoubtedly wish to express this observation. Yet suffering as a discipline is certainly not the whole truth regarding the problem of evil. How could the idea be given its proper weight? Obviously the doctrine could not be placed in the mouth of Job, who denies that there is any justice in suffering. Nor could it be presented by the friends, for the author wishes to negate their standpoint, as we have seen. Finally, were this idea included in the subsequent God speeches, it would weaken the force of the principal answer. By creating the character of Elihu, who opposes the attitude of the friends, as well as that of Job, the author is able to express this secondary idea, giving it due place in his world view.

VIII

Elihu's words end as a storm is seen rising in the east. The Lord Himself appears in the whirlwind and speaks to Job. The argumentation of the friends that Job must be a sinner is treated with the

---

[18] Eliphaz had briefly referred to the idea of suffering as a discipline in one verse (Job 5:16), but had not referred to it again or explored its implications. Deutero-Isaiah's doctrine of the Servant of the Lord describes the Servant's suffering as inflicted by other men, not as emanating directly from God. The affinities are, however, noteworthy.

silence it deserves. Nowhere does God refer to Job's alleged misdoings. Instead, the entire problem is raised to another dimension. Can Job comprehend, let alone govern, the universe that he weighs and finds wanting? Earth and sea, cloud and darkness and dawn, snow and hail, rain and thunder, snow and ice, and the stars above—all these wonders are beyond Job. Nor do these exhaust God's power. With a vividness born of deep love and careful observation, the poet pictures the beasts, remote from man, yet precious to their Maker. The lion and the mountain goat, the wild ass and the buffalo, the ostrich, the horse, and the hawk, all testify to the glory of God. For all their variety, these creatures have one element in common—they are not under the sway of man, or even intended for his use. Even the ponderous hippopotamus and the fearsome crocodile, far from conventionally beautiful, reveal the creative power of God and His joy in the world. Moreover, God declares, were Job able to destroy evil in the world, even He would be prepared to relinquish His throne to him—a moving acknowledgment by God that the world order is not perfect!

Job is not overwhelmed, as is often alleged, by God's physical power. For that had failed to cow Job into silence during the earlier debate with the friends. It is the essential truth of God's position that impels Job to submit. His surrender, however, is still a victory, for his wish has been granted:

> I had heard of Thee by the hearing of the ear,
> But now mine eye seeth Thee;
> Wherefore I abhor my words, and repent,
> Seeing I am dust and ashes
>
> (Job 42:5, 6).

Job's triumph lies in the fact that God speaks to him and does not ignore him. The confrontation of God is Job's vindication.

But that is not all. In rebelling against tradition because of his experience, Job has enriched tradition, for religious truth, like all truth, can grow only through the evidence derived from the experience of life. To use the language of the hour, Job's protest is existential, but it contributes to a deeper essential religion. It compels a reconsideration of the conventional theology, which the author incidentally does not reject out of hand; he merely regards it as inadequate. The author's positive ideas, one major, the other minor, are stated in the two closing sections of the book.

The minor thought is expressed by Elihu, who stresses that suffering frequently serves as a source of moral discipline and is thus a spur to high ethical attainment.

The principal idea is reserved for the God speeches, where the implications, in accordance with widespread Semitic usage, are [19] at least as important as their explicit content.

The vivid and joyous description of nature in these chapters testifies that nature is more than a mystery; it is a cosmos, a thing of beauty. The force of the analogy is not lost upon Job. Just as there is order and harmony in the natural world, so there is order and meaning in the moral sphere. Man cannot fathom the meaning of the natural order, yet he is aware of its beauty and harmony. Similarly, if he cannot expect to comprehend the moral order, he must believe that there is rationality and justice within it. As Kant pointed out, if it is arrogant to defend God, it is even more arrogant to assail Him. After all legitimate explanations of suffering are taken into account, a mystery still remains. Any view of the universe that fully explains it, is on that very account, untrue. The analogy of the natural order gives the believer in God the grounds for facing the mystery with a courage born of faith in the essential rightness of things. What cannot be comprehended through reason must be embraced in love. For the author of Job, as for Judaism always, God is one and indivisible. As nature is instinct with morality, so the moral order is rooted in the natural world.

One other significant contribution to religion emerges from the Book of Job. For the poet, the harmony of the universe is important, not only as an idea but as an experience, not only logically but esthetically. When man steeps himself in the beauty of the world, his troubles grow petty, not because they are unreal, but because they

---

[19] I plan to discuss elsewhere the literary phenomenon of "allusions," which is frequent in Arabic and medieval Hebrew poetry and which has not been adequately reckoned with in biblical poetry.

dissolve within the larger plan, like the tiny dabs of oil in a masterpiece of painting. The beauty of the world becomes an anodyne to man's suffering.

The author of Job is not merely a great artist and poet. He is too deep a religious thinker to believe that any neatly articulated system of man can comprehend the beauty and the tragedy of existence. Yet he is too great an intellect to abdicate the use of reason and reflection in pondering on the mystery of evil and comprehending as much of it as we can. He would endorse the unemotional words of the third century sage, Jannai: "It is not in our power to understand the suffering of the righteous or the well-being of the wicked" (*Aboth* 4:15). There is a residuum of the Unknown in the world, but we have good grounds for holding fast to the faith that harmony and beauty pervade God's world. The mystery is also a miracle.

When Job found that the tradition of the past was contradicted by his personal experience, he resisted the temptation to submit to the platitudes of the past. Because of his unswerving allegiance to the truth, he refused to echo accepted truths, however respectable and ancient their source. His steadfastness and agony found their reward —for out of his suffering emerged a deeper vision of the Eternal and His ways.

CONTRIBUTORS TO "GREAT MORAL DILEMMAS: IN LITERATURE, PAST AND PRESENT" *

ROBERT BIERSTEDT, Ph.D., Columbia University; Professor and Chairman, Department of Sociology, The College of the City of New York.

EDWARD DAVISON, M.A., University of Cambridge, Litt.D., h.c., University of Colorado; Professor of English and Director, School of General Studies, Hunter College of the City of New York.

CHARLES FRANKEL, Ph.D., Columbia University; Associate Professor of Philosophy, Columbia University.

ROBERT GORDIS, Ph.D., Dropsie College, Rabbi, D.D., The Jewish Theological Seminary of America; Associate Professor of Biblical Exegesis, The Jewish Theological Seminary of America; Adjunct Professor of Religion, Columbia University; Author: *Wisdom to Ecclesiastes, Conservative Judaism—An American Philosophy, Koheleth, The Man and His World, The Song of Songs,* and others.

HENRY HATFIELD, Ph.D., Columbia University; Associate Professor, Department of Germanic Languages and Literature, Harvard University.

EDGAR JOHNSON, A.B., Columbia University; Professor of English and Chairman of the Department, The College of the City of New York.

R. M. MACIVER, D. Phil., Edinburgh University, D. Litt., Columbia University, Harvard University; Lieber Professor Emeritus of Political Philosophy and Sociology, Columbia University; Vice President, Conference on Science, Philosophy and Religion; Member, Executive Committee, The Institute for Religious and Social Studies; Author: *The Web of Government, The More Perfect Union, The Ramparts We Guard, Democracy and the Economic Challenge,* and others; Editor: *Group Relations and Group Antagonisms, Civilization and Group Relationships, Unity and Difference in American Life, Discrimination and National Welfare, Great Expressions of Human Rights, Conflict of Loyalties, Moments of Personal Discovery, The Hour of Insight, New Horizons in Creative Thinking: A Survey and Forecast;* Co-Editor: *Symposia of the Conference on Science, Philosophy and Religion.*

* As of October, 1954.

RICHARD McKEON, Ph.D., Columbia University; Charles F. Grey Distinguished Service Professor of Philosophy and Greek, The University of Chicago; Author: *The Philosophy of Spinoza, Freedom and History,* and others.

WHITNEY J. OATES, Ph.D., Princeton University; Chairman, Special Program in the Humanities, Princeton University; Author: *The Complete Greek Drama* (with E. G. O'Neill, Jr.), *The Stoic and Epicurean Philosophers, Greek Literature in Translation* (with C. T. Murphy), *Greek and Roman Classics in Translation* (with C. T. Murphy and K. Guinagh), and others.

JOHN F. C. RICHARDS, Ph.D., Harvard University; Assistant Professor of Greek and Latin, Columbia University.

GEORGE N. SHUSTER, Ph.D., Columbia University; President, Hunter College of the City of New York.

JOHN E. SMITH, B.D., Union Theological Seminary, Ph.D., Columbia University; Assistant Professor of Philosophy, Yale University.

WILLIAM YORK TINDALL, Ph.D., Columbia University; Professor of English, Columbia University; Author: *D. H. Lawrence and Susan, His Cow, Forces in Modern British Literature, James Joyce,* and others.

LIONEL TRILLING, Ph.D., Columbia University; Professor of English, Columbia University; Author: *Matthew Arnold, E. M. Forster, The Middle of the Journey, The Liberal Imagination,* and others.

INDEX